초등에서
브릿지
BRIDGE VOCA
보카
중등으로
Basic

How to Use 브릿지 보카

① 단어 학습과 Daily Test

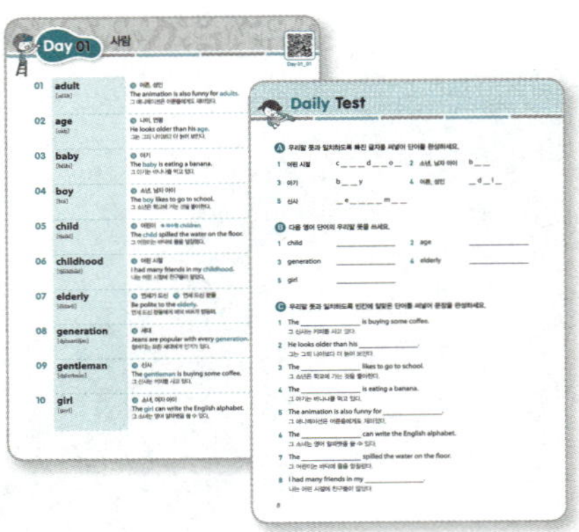

하나의 Day는 20단어로 구성되어 있습니다.
암기 부담을 줄이기 위해 10단어씩 나누어 학습합니다.
원어민의 발음으로 녹음된 단어와 예문을
QR코드를 통해 들으면서 정확한 발음을 익히고,
문장 활용 능력을 키울 수 있습니다.

② Review

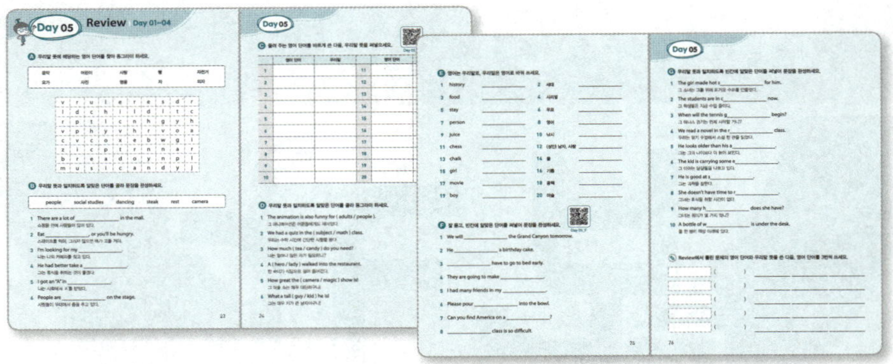

4일 학습 후 5일째에는 지금까지 배운 단어들을 확실하게 복습합니다. Word Search, 문장 완성하기,
받아쓰기 등 다양한 유형의 문제를 풀면서 단어들을 다시 한 번 머릿속에 새깁니다.

③ Index

단어들을 알파벳 순으로 수록하여,
특정 단어를 빠르게 찾을 수 있습니다.

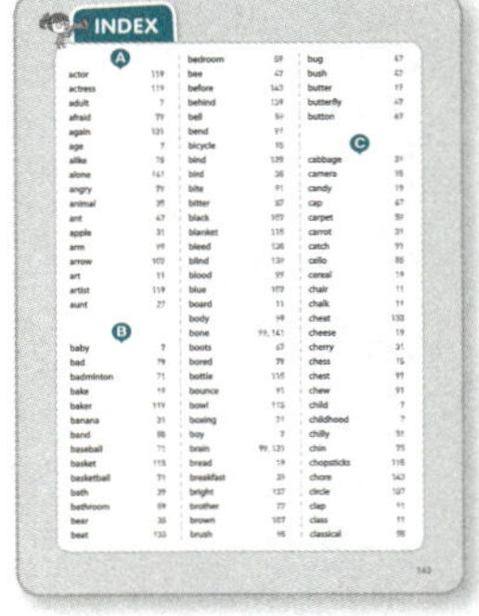

 이 교재의 모든 음원은 메가북스 홈페이지에서
무료 MP3 파일로도 다운받을 수 있습니다.

Contents와 학습 진도표

Day	권 구성	Basic	Intermediate	Advanced
01		사람	음식	활동
02		수업	동물과 식물	사물 묘사
03		취미와 여가	여행과 휴가	문화
04		음식	쇼핑	정치
05		Review	Review	Review
06		가족	장소	자연환경
07		과일과 채소	대인 관계	상황 묘사
08		동물	학교	우주와 과학
09		일상생활	나라와 지역	경제
10		Review	Review	Review
11		식물과 곤충	순서	일의 진행
12		날씨	건물과 건축물	국제 사회
13		음악	가정	상태
14		집	사회생활	생각과 인지
15	주제	Review	Review	Review
16		패션	시장	인물 묘사
17		운동	건강과 질병	위치와 방향
18		얼굴과 인물 묘사	의사소통	달력
19		감정	때와 시기	의견
20		Review	Review	Review
21		감각	크기	교통
22		움직임과 동작	안전과 사고	감정
23		미술	요일과 계절	제작과 판매
24		신체	자연 현상	동네와 길 찾기
25		Review	Review	Review
26		모양과 색깔	성격	행사와 시간
27		숫자	직업	능력
28		생활용품	얼굴과 인물 묘사	대중문화
29		직업	회사	필수 부사
30		Review	Review	Review
31		-ail, -ain	bl-, cl-, fl-, pl-	-ar-
32		-eat, -eed	cr-, dr-, fr-	-er
33	Phonics	-ight, -ind	sk-, sm-, sn-, sp-	-ir-
34		-one, -ore	kn-, -gn, -mb, wr-	-or-, -ur-
35		Review	Review	Review

Day 01~30

오늘 외운 단어를 내일은 몇 개나 기억할 수 있을까요?
하나의 주제와 연관된 단어들을 모아서
의미를 이해하며 외워 보세요.
단어들이 꼬리에 꼬리를 물고 연상되어
오래 기억할 수 있어요.
24가지 주제에 따라 구분된 480단어를
머릿속에 쏙쏙 넣어 보세요.

하나 더! 철저한 복습으로 잊혀져 가는 단어를
확실하게 내 것으로 만들어요.

Day 01 　사람

01　**adult**
[ədʌ́lt]

❸ 어른, 성인
The animation is also funny for adults.
그 애니메이션은 어른들에게도 재미있다.

02　**age**
[eidʒ]

❸ 나이, 연령
He looks older than his age.
그는 그의 나이보다 더 늙어 보인다.

03　**baby**
[béibi]

❸ 아기
The baby is eating a banana.
그 아기는 바나나를 먹고 있다.

04　**boy**
[bɔi]

❸ 소년, 남자 아이
The boy likes to go to school.
그 소년은 학교에 가는 것을 좋아한다.

05　**child**
[tʃaild]

❸ 어린이　✿ 복수형 children
The child spilled the water on the floor.
그 어린이는 바닥에 물을 엎질렀다.

06　**childhood**
[tʃáildhùd]

❸ 어린 시절
I had many friends in my childhood.
나는 어린 시절에 친구들이 많았다.

07　**elderly**
[éldərli]

❹ 연세가 드신　❸ 연세 드신 분들
Be polite to the elderly.
연세 드신 분들에게 예의 바르게 행동해.

08　**generation**
[dʒènəréiʃən]

❸ 세대
Jeans are popular with every generation.
청바지는 모든 세대에게 인기가 있다.

09　**gentleman**
[dʒéntlmən]

❸ 신사
The gentleman is buying some coffee.
그 신사는 커피를 사고 있다.

10　**girl**
[gəːrl]

❸ 소녀, 여자 아이
The girl can write the English alphabet.
그 소녀는 영어 알파벳을 쓸 수 있다.

A 우리말 뜻과 일치하도록 빠진 글자를 써넣어 단어를 완성하세요.

1 어린 시절　　　c _ _ _ d _ _ o _　　**2** 소년, 남자 아이　　b _ _

3 아기　　　b _ _ y　　**4** 어른, 성인　　_ d _ l _

5 신사　　　_ e _ _ _ _ m _ _

B 다음 영어 단어의 우리말 뜻을 쓰세요.

1 child　　_______________　　**2** age　　_______________

3 generation　　_______________　　**4** elderly　　_______________

5 girl　　_______________

C 우리말 뜻과 일치하도록 빈칸에 알맞은 단어를 써넣어 문장을 완성하세요.

1 The _______________ is buying some coffee.
그 신사는 커피를 사고 있다.

2 He looks older than his _______________.
그는 그의 나이보다 더 늙어 보인다.

3 The _______________ likes to go to school.
그 소년은 학교에 가는 것을 좋아한다.

4 The _______________ is eating a banana.
그 아기는 바나나를 먹고 있다.

5 The animation is also funny for _______________.
그 애니메이션은 어른들에게도 재미있다.

6 The _______________ can write the English alphabet.
그 소녀는 영어 알파벳을 쓸 수 있다.

7 The _______________ spilled the water on the floor.
그 어린이는 바닥에 물을 엎질렀다.

8 I had many friends in my _______________.
나는 어린 시절에 친구들이 많았다.

11 guest [gest]
- 명 손님, 투숙객
- What time did the guest arrive?
- 그 손님은 몇 시에 도착했니?

12 guy [gai]
- 명 남자, 녀석
- What a tall guy he is!
- 그는 매우 키가 큰 남자이구나!

13 hero [hí(:)ərou]
- 명 영웅
- The movie is about a true hero.
- 그 영화는 진정한 영웅에 관한 것이다.

14 kid [kid]
- 명 아이
- Kids have to go to bed early.
- 아이들은 일찍 잠자리에 들어야 한다.

15 lady [léidi]
- 명 숙녀, 여성
- A lady walked into the restaurant.
- 한 숙녀가 식당으로 걸어 들어갔다.

16 man [mæn]
- 명 (성인) 남자, 사람
- The young man is standing behind the tree.
- 그 젊은 남자는 나무 뒤에 서 있다.

17 people [pí:pl]
- 명 사람들
- There are a lot of people in the mall.
- 쇼핑몰 안에 사람들이 많이 있다.

18 person [pə́:rsən]
- 명 (개개의) 사람, 개인
- Mike is a warm and friendly person.
- Mike는 따뜻하고 친절한 사람이다.

19 teenager [tí:nèidʒər]
- 명 십 대
- The teenager studied very hard.
- 그 십 대는 매우 열심히 공부했다.

20 woman [wúmən]
- 명 (성인) 여자
- I talked with the woman on the phone.
- 나는 전화로 그 여자와 이야기했다.

Daily Test

A 우리말 뜻과 일치하도록 빠진 글자를 써넣어 단어를 완성하세요.

1 숙녀, 여성 __ a __ y **2** 사람들 p __ __ __ __ e

3 십 대 t __ __ n __ __ __ __ **4** 영웅 __ e __ o

5 (성인) 남자, 사람 m __ __

B 다음 영어 단어의 우리말 뜻을 쓰세요.

1 person _______________ **2** guy _______________

3 kid _______________ **4** woman _______________

5 guest _______________

C 우리말 뜻과 일치하도록 빈칸에 알맞은 단어를 써넣어 문장을 완성하세요.

1 A _______________ walked into the restaurant.
한 숙녀가 식당으로 걸어 들어갔다.

2 The movie is about a true _______________.
그 영화는 진정한 영웅에 관한 것이다.

3 Mike is a warm and friendly _______________.
Mike는 따뜻하고 친절한 사람이다.

4 The _______________ studied very hard.
그 십 대는 매우 열심히 공부했다.

5 The young _______________ is standing behind the tree.
그 젊은 남자는 나무 뒤에 서 있다.

6 There are a lot of _______________ in the mall.
쇼핑몰 안에 사람들이 많이 있다.

7 What time did the _______________ arrive?
그 손님은 몇 시에 도착했니?

8 I talked with the _______________ on the phone.
나는 전화로 그 여자와 이야기했다.

Day 02 수업

01 art
[ɑːrt]

명 미술
What do you do in the art class?
너희는 미술 수업에서 무엇을 하니?

02 board
[bɔːrd]

명 칠판
The child is writing on the board.
그 어린이는 칠판에 쓰고 있다.

03 chair
[tʃɛər]

명 의자
We have to move the chairs.
우리는 그 의자들을 옮겨야 한다.

04 chalk
[tʃɔːk]

명 분필
The teacher dropped the chalk.
그 선생님은 분필을 떨어뜨렸다.

05 class
[klæs]

명 학급, 수업 ✿ in class 수업 중인
The students are in class now.
그 학생들은 지금 수업 중이다.

06 dictionary
[díkʃənèri]

명 사전
You must bring your dictionary.
너는 너의 사전을 가져와야 한다.

07 English
[íŋgliʃ]

명 영어
We have English class twice a week.
우리는 일주일에 두 번 영어 수업이 있다.

08 eraser
[iréisər]

명 지우개
Let's share my eraser.
나의 지우개를 함께 쓰자.

09 globe
[gloub]

명 지구본
Can you find America on a globe?
너는 지구본에서 미국을 찾을 수 있니?

10 history
[hístəri]

명 역사
I have to do my history homework.
나는 나의 역사 숙제를 해야 한다.

Daily Test

A 우리말 뜻과 일치하도록 빠진 글자를 써넣어 단어를 완성하세요.

1 학급, 수업　　　__ l __ __ s

2 칠판　　　__ o a __ __

3 미술　　　a __ __

4 지우개　　　__ __ a __ e __

5 역사　　　h __ s __ __ __ __ __

B 다음 영어 단어의 우리말 뜻을 쓰세요.

1 chair　　　_________________

2 dictionary　　　_________________

3 globe　　　_________________

4 chalk　　　_________________

5 English　　　_________________

C 우리말 뜻과 일치하도록 빈칸에 알맞은 단어를 써넣어 문장을 완성하세요.

1 What do you do in the _________________ class?
너희는 미술 수업에서 무엇을 하니?

2 Let's share my _________________.
나의 지우개를 함께 쓰자.

3 You must bring your _________________.
너는 너의 사전을 가져와야 한다.

4 The child is writing on the _________________.
그 어린이는 칠판에 쓰고 있다.

5 I have to do my _________________ homework.
나는 나의 역사 숙제를 해야 한다.

6 The students are in _________________ now.
그 학생들은 지금 수업 중이다.

7 We have to move the _________________.
우리는 그 의자들을 옮겨야 한다.

8 Can you find America on a _________________?
너는 지구본에서 미국을 찾을 수 있니?

Day 02　수업

11 listening
[lísniŋ]
명 듣기
Listening class is so difficult.
듣기 수업은 너무 어렵다.

12 math
[mæθ]
명 수학
We had a quiz in the math class.
우리는 수학 시간에 간단한 시험을 봤다.

13 music
[mjúːzik]
명 음악
Music class begins at 9 o'clock.
음악 수업은 9시 정각에 시작한다.

14 notebook
[nóutbùk]
명 공책
How much is this notebook?
이 공책은 얼마니?

15 reading
[ríːdiŋ]
명 읽기
We read a novel in the reading class.
우리는 읽기 수업에서 소설 한 편을 읽었다.

16 ruler
[rúːlər]
명 자
Where is my ruler?
나의 자는 어디에 있니?

17 science
[sáiəns]
명 과학
He is good at science.
그는 과학을 잘한다.

18 social studies
[sóuʃəlstʌ̀diːz]
명 사회
I got an "A" in social studies.
나는 사회에서 'A'를 받았다.

19 subject
[sʌ́bdʒikt]
명 학과, 과목
Which subject do you like?
너는 어느 과목을 좋아하니?

20 textbook
[tékstbùk]
명 교과서
Reading textbooks is very helpful.
교과서를 읽는 것은 매우 도움이 된다.

Daily Test

A 우리말 뜻과 일치하도록 빠진 글자를 써넣어 단어를 완성하세요.

1 과학　　　　　s __ __ __ n __ __

2 수학　　　　　m __ __ __

3 학과, 과목　　__ __ __ j __ c __

4 공책　　　　　__ __ t __ __ o __ __

5 읽기　　　　　r __ a __ __ __ __

B 다음 영어 단어의 우리말 뜻을 쓰세요.

1 textbook　　_________________

2 listening　　_________________

3 ruler　　_________________

4 music　　_________________

5 social studies　　_________________

C 우리말 뜻과 일치하도록 빈칸에 알맞은 단어를 써넣어 문장을 완성하세요.

1 How much is this _________________?
이 공책은 얼마니?

2 Where is my _________________?
나의 자는 어디에 있니?

3 _________________ class is so difficult.
듣기 수업은 너무 어렵다.

4 Which _________________ do you like?
너는 어느 과목을 좋아하니?

5 He is good at _________________.
그는 과학을 잘한다.

6 We read a novel in the _________________ class.
우리는 읽기 수업에서 소설 한 편을 읽었다.

7 I got an "A" in _________________.
나는 사회에서 'A'를 받았다.

8 _________________ class begins at 9 o'clock.
음악 수업은 9시 정각에 시작한다.

01	**bicycle** [báisikl]	명 자전거 My brother gave me his old bicycle. 나의 형은 나에게 그의 낡은 자전거를 주었다.
02	**camera** [kǽmərə]	명 카메라 I'm looking for my camera. 나는 나의 카메라를 찾고 있다.
03	**chess** [tʃes]	명 체스 Do you want to play chess with me? 나와 함께 체스를 둘래?
04	**climb** [klaim]	동 오르다, 올라가다 He climbs the mountain every morning. 그는 매일 아침 산을 오른다.
05	**dance** [dæns]	동 춤을 추다　명 춤 People are dancing on the stage. 사람들이 무대에서 춤을 추고 있다.
06	**enjoy** [indʒɔ́i]	동 즐기다 He enjoys reading books. 그는 책 읽는 것을 즐긴다.
07	**fishing** [fíʃiŋ]	명 낚시 Fishing is possible at this lake. 이 호수에서는 낚시가 가능하다.
08	**game** [geim]	명 경기, 게임 When will the tennis game begin? 그 테니스 경기는 언제 시작할 거니?
09	**hobby** [hábi]	명 취미 How many hobbies does she have? 그녀는 취미가 몇 가지 있니?
10	**magic** [mǽdʒik]	명 마술, 마법 How great the magic show is! 그 마술 쇼는 매우 대단하구나!

Daily Test

A 우리말 뜻과 일치하도록 빠진 글자를 써넣어 단어를 완성하세요.

1 카메라   c __ __ __ __ a   **2** 오르다, 올라가다 c __ __ m __

3 낚시   __ __ s __ i __ __   **4** 경기, 게임   g __ __ __

5 자전거   b __ c __ __ __ __

B 다음 영어 단어의 우리말 뜻을 쓰세요.

1 magic ________________ **2** chess ________________

3 hobby ________________ **4** dance ________________

5 enjoy ________________

C 우리말 뜻과 일치하도록 빈칸에 알맞은 단어를 써넣어 문장을 완성하세요.

1 He ________________ the mountain every morning.
그는 매일 아침 산을 오른다.

2 How many ________________ does she have?
그녀는 취미가 몇 가지 있니?

3 How great the ________________ show is!
그 마술 쇼는 매우 대단하구나!

4 People are ________________ on the stage.
사람들이 무대에서 춤을 추고 있다.

5 Do you want to play ________________ with me?
나와 함께 체스를 둘래?

6 I'm looking for my ________________.
나는 나의 카메라를 찾고 있다.

7 He ________________ reading books.
그는 책 읽는 것을 즐긴다.

8 My brother gave me his old ________________.
나의 형은 나에게 그의 낡은 자전거를 주었다.

11 movie
[múːvi]
명 영화
I like to watch a movie alone.
나는 혼자 영화 보는 것을 좋아한다.

12 photo
[fóutou]
명 사진
I found a photo album.
나는 사진첩 하나를 발견했다.

13 relax
[riláeks]
동 휴식을 취하다
She doesn't have time to relax.
그녀는 휴식을 취할 시간이 없다.

14 rest
[rest]
명 휴식　✿ take a rest 휴식을 취하다
He had better take a rest.
그는 휴식을 취하는 것이 좋겠다.

15 shopping
[ʃápiŋ]
명 쇼핑
They don't like shopping.
그들은 쇼핑을 좋아하지 않는다.

16 stamp
[stæmp]
명 우표
Are there any stamps in the box?
상자 안에 우표가 있니?

17 stay
[stei]
동 머무르다
My friend will stay here for five days.
나의 친구는 5일 동안 여기에서 머무를 것이다.

18 surf
[səːrf]
동 파도타기를 하다
They went surfing last summer.
그들은 지난여름에 파도타기를 하러 갔다.

19 visit
[vízit]
동 방문하다　명 방문
We will visit the Grand Canyon tomorrow.
우리는 내일 그랜드 캐니언을 방문할 것이다.

20 yoga
[jóugə]
명 요가
It is time to do yoga.
요가를 할 시간이다.

Daily Test

A 우리말 뜻과 일치하도록 빠진 글자를 써넣어 단어를 완성하세요.

1 휴식을 취하다　　r＿＿a＿　　　　**2** 영화　　　　＿＿v＿e

3 요가　　　　＿o＿＿　　　　　　**4** 머무르다　　＿t＿＿

5 쇼핑　　　　s＿＿＿p＿＿＿

B 다음 영어 단어의 우리말 뜻을 쓰세요.

1 rest　　＿＿＿＿＿＿＿＿　　　　**2** visit　　＿＿＿＿＿＿＿＿

3 stamp　　＿＿＿＿＿＿＿＿　　　**4** surf　　＿＿＿＿＿＿＿＿

5 photo　　＿＿＿＿＿＿＿＿

C 우리말 뜻과 일치하도록 빈칸에 알맞은 단어를 써넣어 문장을 완성하세요.

1 They don't like ＿＿＿＿＿＿＿.
그들은 쇼핑을 좋아하지 않는다.

2 It is time to do ＿＿＿＿＿＿＿.
요가를 할 시간이다.

3 He had better take a ＿＿＿＿＿＿＿.
그는 휴식을 취하는 것이 좋겠다.

4 I like to watch a ＿＿＿＿＿＿＿ alone.
나는 혼자 영화 보는 것을 좋아한다.

5 We will ＿＿＿＿＿＿＿ the Grand Canyon tomorrow.
우리는 내일 그랜드 캐니언을 방문할 것이다.

6 My friend will ＿＿＿＿＿＿＿ here for five days.
나의 친구는 5일 동안 여기에서 머무를 것이다.

7 I found a ＿＿＿＿＿＿＿ album.
나는 사진첩 하나를 발견했다.

8 Are there any ＿＿＿＿＿＿＿ in the box?
상자 안에 우표가 있니?

Day 04_01

01　bake
[beik]
동 굽다
He baked a birthday cake.
그는 생일 케이크를 구웠다.

02　bread
[bred]
명 빵
We eat bread for breakfast.
우리는 아침으로 빵을 먹는다.

03　butter
[bʌ́tər]
명 버터
There is not any butter on the shelf.
선반에 버터가 하나도 없다.

04　candy
[kǽndi]
명 사탕
The boy has a box of candy.
그 소년은 사탕 한 상자를 가지고 있다.

05　cereal
[síriəl]
명 시리얼
Ann buys two bags of cereal.
Ann은 시리얼 두 봉지를 산다.

06　cheese
[tʃiːz]
명 치즈
I eat three slices of cheese.
나는 치즈 세 조각을 먹는다.

07　cookie
[kúki]
명 쿠키
The chocolate cookies are theirs.
그 초콜릿 쿠키들은 그들의 것이다.

08　egg
[eg]
명 달걀, 알
The kid is carrying some eggs.
그 아이는 달걀들을 나르고 있다.

09　food
[fuːd]
명 음식, 식량
Everyone will bring some food.
모든 사람이 음식을 가져올 것이다.

10　honey
[hʌ́ni]
명 꿀
This honey tastes very sweet.
이 꿀은 매우 달콤한 맛이 난다.

Daily Test

A 우리말 뜻과 일치하도록 빠진 글자를 써넣어 단어를 완성하세요.

1 굽다   __ __ k __

2 치즈   c __ __ e __ __

3 음식, 식량   __ __ o __

4 달걀, 알   __ g __

5 버터   __ u __ __ e __

B 다음 영어 단어의 우리말 뜻을 쓰세요.

1 honey   _________________

2 bread   _________________

3 candy   _________________

4 cereal   _________________

5 cookie   _________________

C 우리말 뜻과 일치하도록 빈칸에 알맞은 단어를 써넣어 문장을 완성하세요.

1 There is not any _________________ on the shelf.
선반에 버터가 하나도 없다.

2 We eat _________________ for breakfast.
우리는 아침으로 빵을 먹는다.

3 I eat three slices of _________________.
나는 치즈 세 조각을 먹는다.

4 Ann buys two bags of _________________.
Ann은 시리얼 두 봉지를 산다.

5 The chocolate _________________ are theirs.
그 초콜릿 쿠키들은 그들의 것이다.

6 He _________________ a birthday cake.
그는 생일 케이크를 구웠다.

7 This _________________ tastes very sweet.
이 꿀은 매우 달콤한 맛이 난다.

8 The boy has a box of _________________.
그 소년은 사탕 한 상자를 가지고 있다.

11 jam
[dʒæm]

명 잼

They are going to make jam.
그들은 잼을 만들 것이다.

12 juice
[dʒuːs]

명 주스

Which do you want, juice or Coke?
너희는 주스와 콜라 중 어느 것을 원하니?

13 meat
[miːt]

명 고기

The man isn't eating meat.
그 남자는 고기를 먹고 있지 않다.

14 milk
[milk]

명 우유

Please pour milk into the bowl.
그릇에 우유를 부어 주세요.

15 oil
[ɔil]

명 기름

Do not use the oil.
그 기름을 사용하지 마.

16 pizza
[píːtsə]

명 피자

The pizza is delicious but expensive.
그 피자는 맛있지만 비싸다.

17 soup
[suːp]

명 수프

The girl made hot soup for him.
그 소녀는 그를 위해 뜨거운 수프를 만들었다.

18 steak
[steik]

명 스테이크

Eat steak, or you'll be hungry.
스테이크를 먹어, 그러지 않으면 배가 고플 거야.

19 tea
[tiː]

명 차

How much tea do you need?
너는 얼마나 많은 차가 필요하니?

20 water
[wɔ́ːtər]

명 물　동 물을 주다

A bottle of water is under the desk.
물 한 병이 책상 아래에 있다.

Daily Test

A 우리말 뜻과 일치하도록 빠진 글자를 써넣어 단어를 완성하세요.

1 피자   p __ __ __ a   **2** 주스   __ __ i __ e

3 물; 물을 주다   __ a __ __ __   **4** 우유   __ __ __ k

5 수프   __ o __ __

B 다음 영어 단어의 우리말 뜻을 쓰세요.

1 meat   __________________   **2** oil   __________________

3 steak   __________________   **4** tea   __________________

5 jam   __________________

C 우리말 뜻과 일치하도록 빈칸에 알맞은 단어를 써넣어 문장을 완성하세요.

1 The girl made hot _________________ for him.
그 소녀는 그를 위해 뜨거운 수프를 만들었다.

2 Eat _________________, or you'll be hungry.
스테이크를 먹어, 그러지 않으면 배가 고플 거야.

3 Please pour _________________ into the bowl.
그릇에 우유를 부어 주세요.

4 A bottle of _________________ is under the desk.
물 한 병이 책상 아래에 있다.

5 The _________________ is delicious but expensive.
그 피자는 맛있지만 비싸다.

6 Which do you want, _________________ or Coke?
너희는 주스와 콜라 중 어느 것을 원하니?

7 They are going to make _________________.
그들은 잼을 만들 것이다.

8 The man isn't eating _________________.
그 남자는 고기를 먹고 있지 않다.

A 우리말 뜻에 해당하는 영어 단어를 찾아 동그라미 하세요.

음악	어린이	사탕	빵	자전거
요가	사진	영웅	자	의자

v	r	u	l	e	r	e	s	d	r
l	d	c	h	i	l	d	l	t	c
r	p	t	l	c	n	h	g	y	h
v	p	h	y	v	h	r	v	o	a
c	v	c	o	x	e	b	w	g	i
z	i	c	p	t	r	n	n	a	r
b	r	e	a	d	o	y	n	p	l
m	u	s	i	c	a	n	d	y	j

B 우리말 뜻과 일치하도록 알맞은 단어를 골라 문장을 완성하세요.

people	social studies	dancing	steak	rest	camera

1 There are a lot of ________________ in the mall.
쇼핑몰 안에 사람들이 많이 있다.

2 Eat ________________, or you'll be hungry.
스테이크를 먹어, 그러지 않으면 배가 고플 거야.

3 I'm looking for my ________________.
나는 나의 카메라를 찾고 있다.

4 He had better take a ________________.
그는 휴식을 취하는 것이 좋겠다.

5 I got an "A" in ________________.
나는 사회에서 'A'를 받았다.

6 People are ________________ on the stage.
사람들이 무대에서 춤을 추고 있다.

C 들려 주는 영어 단어를 바르게 쓴 다음, 우리말 뜻을 써넣으세요.

Day 05_C

	영어 단어	우리말		영어 단어	우리말
1			11		
2			12		
3			13		
4			14		
5			15		
6			16		
7			17		
8			18		
9			19		
10			20		

D 우리말 뜻과 일치하도록 알맞은 단어를 골라 동그라미 하세요.

1 The animation is also funny for (adults / people).
그 애니메이션은 어른들에게도 재미있다.

2 We had a quiz in the (subject / math) class.
우리는 수학 시간에 간단한 시험을 봤다.

3 How much (tea / candy) do you need?
너는 얼마나 많은 차가 필요하니?

4 A (hero / lady) walked into the restaurant.
한 숙녀가 식당으로 걸어 들어갔다.

5 How great the (camera / magic) show is!
그 마술 쇼는 매우 대단하구나!

6 What a tall (guy / kid) he is!
그는 매우 키가 큰 남자이구나!

E 영어는 우리말로, 우리말은 영어로 바꿔 쓰세요.

1	history	__________	2	세대	__________
3	food	__________	4	시리얼	__________
5	stay	__________	6	우표	__________
7	person	__________	8	영어	__________
9	juice	__________	10	낚시	__________
11	chess	__________	12	(성인) 남자, 사람	__________
13	chalk	__________	14	꿀	__________
15	girl	__________	16	기름	__________
17	movie	__________	18	공책	__________
19	boy	__________	20	미술	__________

Day 05_F

F 잘 듣고, 빈칸에 알맞은 단어를 써넣어 문장을 완성하세요.

1 We will __________ the Grand Canyon tomorrow.

2 He __________ a birthday cake.

3 __________ have to go to bed early.

4 They are going to make __________.

5 I had many friends in my __________.

6 Please pour __________ into the bowl.

7 Can you find America on a __________?

8 __________ class is so difficult.

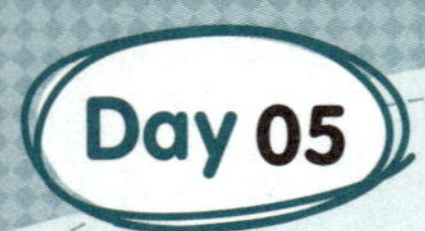

G 우리말 뜻과 일치하도록 빈칸에 알맞은 단어를 써넣어 문장을 완성하세요.

1 The girl made hot s_________________ for him.
그 소녀는 그를 위해 뜨거운 수프를 만들었다.

2 The students are in c_________________ now.
그 학생들은 지금 수업 중이다.

3 When will the tennis g_________________ begin?
그 테니스 경기는 언제 시작할 거니?

4 We read a novel in the r_________________ class.
우리는 읽기 수업에서 소설 한 편을 읽었다.

5 He looks older than his a_________________.
그는 그의 나이보다 더 늙어 보인다.

6 The kid is carrying some e_________________.
그 아이는 달걀들을 나르고 있다.

7 He is good at s_________________.
그는 과학을 잘한다.

8 She doesn't have time to r_________________.
그녀는 휴식을 취할 시간이 없다.

9 How many h_________________ does she have?
그녀는 취미가 몇 가지 있니?

10 A bottle of w_________________ is under the desk.
물 한 병이 책상 아래에 있다.

Review에서 틀린 문제의 영어 단어와 우리말 뜻을 쓴 다음, 영어 단어를 3번씩 쓰세요.

	( )	___________ ___________ ___________
	( )	___________ ___________ ___________
	( )	___________ ___________ ___________
	( )	___________ ___________ ___________
	( )	___________ ___________ ___________

 Day 06 가족

01 aunt [ænt]
명 고모, 이모, 숙모
My aunt showed me her photos.
나의 고모는 나에게 그녀의 사진들을 보여 주었다.

02 brother [brʌðər]
명 형, 오빠, 남동생
When is your brother's birthday?
너의 남동생의 생일은 언제니?

03 cousin [kʌ́zən]
명 사촌
I meet my cousin every Christmas.
나는 크리스마스마다 나의 사촌을 만난다.

04 daughter [dɔ́:tər]
명 딸
I have a six-year-old daughter.
나는 6살 된 딸이 한 명 있다.

05 family [fǽməli]
명 가족
He will talk about his family.
그는 그의 가족에 대해 말할 것이다.

06 father [fɑ́:ðər]
명 아버지
My father can fix the roof.
나의 아버지는 그 지붕을 고치실 수 있다.

07 grandfather [grǽndfɑ̀:ðər]
명 할아버지
Her grandfather was a pilot.
그녀의 할아버지는 비행기 조종사이셨다.

08 grandmother [grǽndmʌ̀ðər]
명 할머니
Does your grandmother cook well?
너의 할머니는 요리를 잘하시니?

09 grandparent [grǽndpɛ̀ərənt]
명 조부모 (중의 한 명)
We often visit our grandparents.
우리는 우리의 조부모님을 자주 방문한다.

10 husband [hʌ́zbənd]
명 남편
Her husband is writing a letter.
그녀의 남편은 편지를 쓰고 있다.

Daily Test

A 우리말 뜻과 일치하도록 빠진 글자를 써넣어 단어를 완성하세요.

1 아버지   f _ _ _ _ r   **2** 할아버지   g r _ _ d _ _ t _ _ r

3 형, 오빠, 남동생   _ _ _ t _ e _   **4** 남편   _ u s _ _ _ _ _

5 할머니   g _ _ _ _ _ _ _ h _ _

B 다음 영어 단어의 우리말 뜻을 쓰세요.

1 family   _______________   **2** cousin   _______________

3 aunt   _______________   **4** daughter   _______________

5 grandparent   _______________

C 우리말 뜻과 일치하도록 빈칸에 알맞은 단어를 써넣어 문장을 완성하세요.

1 Does your _______________ cook well?
너의 할머니는 요리를 잘하시니?

2 My _______________ showed me her photos.
나의 고모는 나에게 그녀의 사진들을 보여 주었다.

3 My _______________ can fix the roof.
나의 아버지는 그 지붕을 고치실 수 있다.

4 He will talk about his _______________.
그는 그의 가족에 대해 말할 것이다.

5 Her _______________ is writing a letter.
그녀의 남편은 편지를 쓰고 있다.

6 I meet my _______________ every Christmas.
나는 크리스마스마다 나의 사촌을 만난다.

7 I have a six-year-old _______________.
나는 6살 된 딸이 한 명 있다.

8 Her _______________ was a pilot.
그녀의 할아버지는 비행기 조종사이셨다.

 Day 06 가족

11 mother
[mʌ́ðər]

명 어머니
My mother cooks for me every day.
나의 어머니는 매일 나를 위해 요리하신다.

12 nephew
[néfjuː]

명 남자 조카
She takes care of her nephew.
그녀는 그녀의 남자 조카를 돌본다.

13 niece
[niːs]

명 여자 조카
My niece is a famous singer.
나의 여자 조카는 유명한 가수이다.

14 parent
[pέ(ː)ərənt]

명 부모 (중의 한 명)
I will have a surprise party for my parents.
나는 나의 부모님을 위해 깜짝 파티를 열 것이다.

15 relative
[rélətiv]

명 친척
Their relatives live in Busan.
그들의 친척들은 부산에 산다.

16 sister
[sístər]

명 언니, 누나, 여동생
Her sister is taller than me.
그녀의 여동생은 나보다 더 키가 크다.

17 son
[sʌn]

명 아들
Is your son at the gym now?
당신의 아들은 지금 체육관에 있나요?

18 twin
[twin]

명 쌍둥이 (중의 한 명)
The twins are wearing the same dress.
그 쌍둥이는 똑같은 원피스를 입고 있다.

19 uncle
[ʌ́ŋkl]

명 삼촌, 이모부, 고모부
His uncle is in the hospital.
그의 삼촌은 병원에 입원해 있다.

20 wife
[waif]

명 아내
His wife works in a bank.
그의 아내는 은행에서 일한다.

Daily Test

A 우리말 뜻과 일치하도록 빠진 글자를 써넣어 단어를 완성하세요.

1 아들   __ __ n

2 여자 조카   n __ e __ __

3 쌍둥이 (중의 한 명) __ w __ __

4 부모 (중의 한 명)   p __ __ __ n __

5 아내   w __ __ __

B 다음 영어 단어의 우리말 뜻을 쓰세요.

1 nephew   _______________

2 uncle   _______________

3 relative   _______________

4 sister   _______________

5 mother   _______________

C 우리말 뜻과 일치하도록 빈칸에 알맞은 단어를 써넣어 문장을 완성하세요.

1 My _______________ is a famous singer.
나의 여자 조카는 유명한 가수이다.

2 Is your _______________ at the gym now?
당신의 아들은 지금 체육관에 있나요?

3 The _______________ are wearing the same dress.
그 쌍둥이는 똑같은 원피스를 입고 있다.

4 She takes care of her _______________.
그녀는 그녀의 남자 조카를 돌본다.

5 His _______________ works in a bank.
그의 아내는 은행에서 일한다.

6 Their _______________ live in Busan.
그들의 친척들은 부산에 산다.

7 My _______________ cooks for me every day.
나의 어머니는 매일 나를 위해 요리하신다.

8 Her _______________ is taller than me.
그녀의 여동생은 나보다 더 키가 크다.

Day 07 — 과일과 채소

01 apple
[ǽpl]
명 사과
Those apples taste sour.
저 사과들은 신맛이 난다.

02 banana
[bənǽnə]
명 바나나
The men pick bananas.
그 남자들은 바나나를 딴다.

03 cabbage
[kǽbidʒ]
명 양배추
This is our cabbage field.
이곳은 우리의 양배추 밭이다.

04 carrot
[kǽrət]
명 당근
You don't have to cut a carrot.
너는 당근을 자를 필요가 없다.

05 cherry
[tʃéri]
명 체리
They have a few cherries.
그들은 체리를 몇 개 가지고 있다.

06 corn
[kɔːrn]
명 옥수수
Mix corn and milk.
옥수수와 우유를 섞어.

07 eggplant
[égplæ̀nt]
명 가지
My brother hates eggplants.
나의 형은 가지를 몹시 싫어한다.

08 fruit
[fruːt]
명 과일
Fresh fruits are good for dessert.
신선한 과일은 후식으로 좋다.

09 garlic
[gáːrlik]
명 마늘
Garlic has a strong smell.
마늘은 강한 냄새를 가지고 있다.

10 grape
[greip]
명 포도
We are washing grapes together.
우리는 함께 포도를 씻고 있다.

Daily Test

A 우리말 뜻과 일치하도록 빠진 글자를 써넣어 단어를 완성하세요.

1 체리 c __ __ r __ __

2 포도 __ __ a __ __

3 사과 __ __ __ l __

4 과일 __ r __ __ t

5 옥수수 __ __ r __

B 다음 영어 단어의 우리말 뜻을 쓰세요.

1 carrot ___________________

2 cabbage ___________________

3 banana ___________________

4 eggplant ___________________

5 garlic ___________________

C 우리말 뜻과 일치하도록 빈칸에 알맞은 단어를 써넣어 문장을 완성하세요.

1 You don't have to cut a _________________.
너는 당근을 자를 필요가 없다.

2 Fresh _________________ are good for dessert.
신선한 과일은 후식으로 좋다.

3 Mix _________________ and milk.
옥수수와 우유를 섞어.

4 This is our _________________ field.
이곳은 우리의 양배추 밭이다.

5 _________________ has a strong smell.
마늘은 강한 냄새를 가지고 있다.

6 Those _________________ taste sour.
저 사과들은 신맛이 난다.

7 We are washing _________________ together.
우리는 함께 포도를 씻고 있다.

8 They have a few _________________.
그들은 체리를 몇 개 가지고 있다.

11 lemon
[lémən]

명 레몬
We will make jam with these lemons.
우리는 이 레몬들로 잼을 만들 것이다.

12 mango
[mǽŋgou]

명 망고
They can eat all the mangoes.
그들은 그 모든 망고들을 먹을 수 있다.

13 mushroom
[mʌ́ʃru(:)m]

명 버섯
You should not touch the mushroom.
너는 그 버섯을 만지지 않는 것이 좋겠다.

14 onion
[ʌ́njən]

명 양파
Look at that huge onion!
저 거대한 양파를 봐!

15 orange
[ɔ́(:)rindʒ]

명 오렌지
The baby likes oranges.
그 아기는 오렌지를 좋아한다.

16 peach
[pi:tʃ]

명 복숭아
We have a peach tree in the yard.
우리 마당에는 복숭아 나무가 한 그루 있다.

17 pear
[pɛər]

명 배
The third pear is not long.
세 번째 배는 길지 않다.

18 pineapple
[páinæ̀pl]

명 파인애플
The pineapple costs ten dollars.
그 파인애플은 10달러이다.

19 potato
[pətéitou]

명 감자
Mom boiled twenty potatoes.
엄마는 감자 스무 개를 삶으셨다.

20 vegetable
[védʒitəbl]

명 채소
Can I use some vegetables?
채소를 좀 사용해도 될까?

A 우리말 뜻과 일치하도록 빠진 글자를 써넣어 단어를 완성하세요.

1 복숭아   __ __ a __ __

2 망고   __ __ n g __

3 감자   p __ __ a __ __

4 오렌지   __ __ a __ g __

5 버섯   __ u __ __ r __ __ __

B 다음 영어 단어의 우리말 뜻을 쓰세요.

1 pineapple _______________

2 vegetable _______________

3 lemon _______________

4 onion _______________

5 pear _______________

C 우리말 뜻과 일치하도록 빈칸에 알맞은 단어를 써넣어 문장을 완성하세요.

1 We have a _______________ tree in the yard.
우리 마당에는 복숭아 나무가 한 그루 있다.

2 We will make jam with these _______________.
우리는 이 레몬들로 잼을 만들 것이다.

3 The third _______________ is not long.
세 번째 배는 길지 않다.

4 They can eat all the _______________.
그들은 그 모든 망고들을 먹을 수 있다.

5 You should not touch the _______________.
너는 그 버섯을 만지지 않는 것이 좋겠다.

6 Can I use some _______________?
채소를 좀 사용해도 될까?

7 The _______________ costs ten dollars.
그 파인애플은 10달러이다.

8 Look at that huge _______________!
저 거대한 양파를 봐!

Day 08　동물

01　animal
[ǽnəməl]

명 동물
There are a lot of animals in the zoo.
동물원에 많은 동물들이 있다.

02　bear
[bɛər]

명 곰
Do bears sleep in winter?
곰은 겨울에 잠을 자니?

03　bird
[bə:rd]

명 새
The bird was the most colorful of the three.
그 새는 그 세 마리 중에서 가장 알록달록했다.

04　duck
[dʌk]

명 오리
All the ducks are on the lake.
그 모든 오리들은 호수에 있다.

05　elephant
[éləfənt]

명 코끼리
Did the elephant break the fence?
그 코끼리가 그 울타리를 부쉈니?

06　frog
[frɔ:g]

명 개구리
A frog can swim well.
개구리는 헤엄을 잘 칠 수 있다.

07　giraffe
[dʒərǽf]

명 기린
The giraffe is five meters tall.
그 기린은 키가 5미터이다.

08　goat
[gout]

명 염소
How long does a goat live?
염소는 얼마나 오래 사니?

09　hen
[hen]

명 암탉
A hen is coming out of the house.
암탉 한 마리가 그 집에서 나오고 있다.

10　horse
[hɔ:rs]

명 말
Which horse is slower?
어느 말이 더 느리니?

Daily Test

A 우리말 뜻과 일치하도록 빠진 글자를 써넣어 단어를 완성하세요.

1 말 　　　　__ __ __ s __

2 곰 　　　　__ __ __ r

3 염소 　　　　__ o __ __

4 기린 　　　　g __ __ __ f __ __

5 동물 　　　　a __ __ __ a __

B 다음 영어 단어의 우리말 뜻을 쓰세요.

1 duck __________________

2 bird __________________

3 hen __________________

4 frog __________________

5 elephant __________________

C 우리말 뜻과 일치하도록 빈칸에 알맞은 단어를 써넣어 문장을 완성하세요.

1 How long does a _______________ live?
염소는 얼마나 오래 사니?

2 Which _______________ is slower?
어느 말이 더 느리니?

3 The _______________ was the most colorful of the three.
그 새는 그 세 마리 중에서 가장 알록달록했다.

4 The _______________ is five meters tall.
그 기린은 키가 5미터이다.

5 All the _______________ are on the lake.
그 모든 오리들은 호수에 있다.

6 Did the _______________ break the fence?
그 코끼리가 그 울타리를 부쉈니?

7 A _______________ is coming out of the house.
암탉 한 마리가 그 집에서 나오고 있다.

8 A _______________ can swim well.
개구리는 헤엄을 잘 칠 수 있다.

11 iguana
[igwá:nə]

명 이구아나
Don't forget to feed the iguana.
그 이구아나에게 먹이 주는 것을 잊지 마.

12 lamb
[læm]

명 새끼 양
The lamb wasn't standing on the field.
그 새끼 양은 풀밭에 서 있지 않았다.

13 lion
[láiən]

명 사자
Lions usually hunt at night.
사자는 보통 밤에 사냥을 한다.

14 monkey
[mʌ́ŋki]

명 원숭이
A monkey has a long tail.
원숭이는 긴 꼬리를 가지고 있다.

15 ox
[ɑks]

명 황소   ✿ 복수형 oxen
The ox can run very fast.
그 황소는 매우 빠르게 달릴 수 있다.

16 pig
[pig]

명 돼지
Whose pigs are those?
저것들은 누구의 돼지니?

17 snake
[sneik]

명 뱀
The snake lives in the Amazon.
그 뱀은 아마존 강에 산다.

18 tiger
[táigər]

명 호랑이
The baby tiger is really cute.
그 새끼 호랑이는 정말 귀엽다.

19 wolf
[wulf]

명 늑대
A wolf is a wild animal.
늑대는 야생 동물이다.

20 zebra
[zí:brə]

명 얼룩말
The zebras are drinking water.
그 얼룩말들은 물을 마시고 있다.

Daily Test

A 우리말 뜻과 일치하도록 빠진 글자를 써넣어 단어를 완성하세요.

1 뱀   _ _ _ k _   **2** 새끼 양   _ a _ _

3 얼룩말   z _ b _ _   **4** 사자   _ _ _ n

5 돼지   _ _ g

B 다음 영어 단어의 우리말 뜻을 쓰세요.

1 monkey   __________   **2** wolf   __________

3 tiger   __________   **4** ox   __________

5 iguana   __________

C 우리말 뜻과 일치하도록 빈칸에 알맞은 단어를 써넣어 문장을 완성하세요.

1 Whose __________ are those?
저것들은 누구의 돼지니?

2 A __________ is a wild animal.
늑대는 야생 동물이다.

3 Don't forget to feed the __________.
그 이구아나에게 먹이 주는 것을 잊지 마.

4 The __________ lives in the Amazon.
그 뱀은 아마존 강에 산다.

5 The __________ can run very fast.
그 황소는 매우 빠르게 달릴 수 있다.

6 The __________ are drinking water.
그 얼룩말들은 물을 마시고 있다.

7 The __________ wasn't standing on the field.
그 새끼 양은 풀밭에 서 있지 않았다.

8 The baby __________ is really cute.
그 새끼 호랑이는 정말 귀엽다.

Day 09 일상생활

01 bath
[bæθ]

명 목욕 ✿ take a bath 목욕을 하다
When will you take a bath?
너는 언제 목욕을 할 거니?

02 breakfast
[brékfəst]

명 아침 식사
I'm going to have breakfast.
나는 아침을 먹을 것이다.

03 clean
[kli:n]

동 닦다, 청소하다 형 깨끗한
We have to clean our room every day.
우리는 매일 우리의 방을 청소해야 한다.

04 clothes
[klouðz]

명 옷, 의복
All the clothes in the store are pretty.
그 가게에 있는 모든 옷들은 예쁘다.

05 diary
[dáiəri]

명 일기 ✿ keep a diary 일기를 쓰다
The girl is keeping a diary.
그 소녀는 일기를 쓰고 있다.

06 dinner
[dínər]

명 저녁 식사
He makes spaghetti for dinner.
그는 저녁 식사로 스파게티를 만든다.

07 drink
[driŋk]

동 마시다 ✿ drink-drank-drunk
What would you like to drink?
무엇을 마시겠습니까?

08 eat
[i:t]

동 먹다 ✿ eat-ate-eaten
Does she eat chocolate after jogging?
그녀는 조깅 후에 초콜릿을 먹니?

09 exercise
[éksərsàiz]

동 운동하다
He often exercises in the playground.
그는 운동장에서 자주 운동을 한다.

10 go out
[gouáut]

동 외출하다
Bill rarely goes out on weekends.
Bill은 주말에 거의 외출하지 않는다.

Daily Test

A 우리말 뜻과 일치하도록 빠진 글자를 써넣어 단어를 완성하세요.

1 일기　　　　d __ a __ __　　　　2 닦다; 깨끗한　　c __ __ a __

3 마시다　　　 __ r __ __ __　　　4 옷, 의복　　　 __ __ o __ h __ __

5 먹다　　　　e __ __

B 다음 영어 단어의 우리말 뜻을 쓰세요.

1 go out　　________________　　2 exercise　　________________

3 dinner　　________________　　4 bath　　________________

5 breakfast　　________________

C 우리말 뜻과 일치하도록 빈칸에 알맞은 단어를 써넣어 문장을 완성하세요.

1 When will you take a ________________?
너는 언제 목욕을 할 거니?

2 He often ________________ in the playground.
그는 운동장에서 자주 운동을 한다.

3 We have to ________________ our room every day.
우리는 매일 우리의 방을 청소해야 한다.

4 Does she ________________ chocolate after jogging?
그녀는 조깅 후에 초콜릿을 먹니?

5 All the ________________ in the store are pretty.
그 가게에 있는 모든 옷들은 예쁘다.

6 The girl is keeping a ________________.
그 소녀는 일기를 쓰고 있다.

7 What would you like to ________________?
무엇을 마시겠습니까?

8 He makes spaghetti for ________________.
그는 저녁 식사로 스파게티를 만든다.

11 homework
[hóumwə̀ːrk]

뗑 숙제
You must do your homework first.
너는 먼저 너의 숙제를 해야 한다.

12 lunch
[lʌntʃ]

뗑 점심 식사
Where are we going to have lunch?
우리는 어디에서 점심을 먹을 거니?

13 meet
[miːt]

똥 만나다 ✿ meet-met-met
They will meet on January 1.
그들은 1월 1일에 만날 것이다.

14 nap
[næp]

뗑 낮잠 ✿ take a nap 낮잠을 자다
I took a nap, but I'm still sleepy.
나는 낮잠을 잤지만, 여전히 졸리다.

15 pet
[pet]

뗑 애완동물
Is the boy playing with his pet?
그 소년은 그의 애완동물과 놀고 있니?

16 sleep
[sliːp]

똥 (잠을) 자다 ✿ sleep-slept-slept
My cat sleeps on the blanket.
나의 고양이는 이불 위에서 잠을 잔다.

17 talk
[tɔːk]

똥 말하다, 이야기하다
She is talking to her teacher.
그녀는 그녀의 선생님에게 말하고 있다.

18 wake up
[weikʌ́p]

똥 깨다, 일어나다
Wake up now, or you'll miss the bus.
지금 일어나, 그러지 않으면 그 버스를 놓칠 거야.

19 wash
[wɑʃ]

똥 씻다
Her son washed his hands.
그녀의 아들은 그의 손을 씻었다.

20 wear
[wɛər]

똥 입다, 신다, 쓰다 ✿ wear-wore-worn
The students wear hats every day.
그 학생들은 매일 모자를 쓴다.

Daily Test

A 우리말 뜻과 일치하도록 빠진 글자를 써넣어 단어를 완성하세요.

1 씻다   __ __ s __

2 애완동물   __ e __

3 입다, 신다, 쓰다   __ __ __ r

4 점심 식사   l __ n __ __

5 숙제   __ __ m __ w __ __ __

B 다음 영어 단어의 우리말 뜻을 쓰세요.

1 meet _________________

2 wake up _________________

3 nap _________________

4 sleep _________________

5 talk _________________

C 우리말 뜻과 일치하도록 빈칸에 알맞은 단어를 써넣어 문장을 완성하세요.

1 I took a _________________, but I'm still sleepy.
나는 낮잠을 잤지만, 여전히 졸리다.

2 The students _________________ hats every day.
그 학생들은 매일 모자를 쓴다.

3 You must do your _________________ first.
너는 먼저 너의 숙제를 해야 한다.

4 Is the boy playing with his _________________?
그 소년은 그의 애완동물과 놀고 있니?

5 She is _________________ to her teacher.
그녀는 그녀의 선생님에게 말하고 있다.

6 Where are we going to have _________________?
우리는 어디에서 점심을 먹을 거니?

7 My cat _________________ on the blanket.
나의 고양이는 이불 위에서 잠을 잔다.

8 They will _________________ on January 1.
그들은 1월 1일에 만날 것이다.

A 우리말 뜻에 해당하는 영어 단어를 찾아 동그라미 하세요.

저녁 식사	개구리	형, 오빠, 남동생	옥수수	만나다
동물	과일	아내	감자	새끼 양

j	p	o	t	a	t	o	x	w	d
f	r	u	i	t	b	p	z	c	i
r	q	q	g	n	j	m	f	o	n
o	f	b	r	o	t	h	e	r	n
g	p	l	q	j	r	y	w	n	e
d	c	j	a	p	d	g	i	r	r
n	a	n	i	m	a	l	f	f	k
m	e	e	t	c	b	l	e	z	f

B 우리말 뜻과 일치하도록 알맞은 단어를 골라 문장을 완성하세요.

breakfast	grapes	wake up	vegetables	nephew	zebras

1 She takes care of her ______________.
그녀는 그녀의 남자 조카를 돌본다.

2 We are washing ______________ together.
우리는 함께 포도를 씻고 있다.

3 The ______________ are drinking water.
그 얼룩말들은 물을 마시고 있다.

4 I'm going to have ______________.
나는 아침을 먹을 것이다.

5 ______________ now, or you'll miss the bus.
지금 일어나, 그러지 않으면 그 버스를 놓칠 거야.

6 Can I use some ______________?
채소를 좀 사용해도 될까?

Day 10

C 들려 주는 영어 단어를 바르게 쓴 다음, 우리말 뜻을 써넣으세요.

Day 10_C

	영어 단어	우리말		영어 단어	우리말
1			11		
2			12		
3			13		
4			14		
5			15		
6			16		
7			17		
8			18		
9			19		
10			20		

D 우리말 뜻과 일치하도록 알맞은 단어를 골라 동그라미 하세요.

1 The students (wear / meet) hats every day.
그 학생들은 매일 모자를 쓴다.

2 I will have a surprise party for my (relatives / parents).
나는 나의 부모님을 위해 깜짝 파티를 열 것이다.

3 Do (bears / hens) sleep in winter?
곰은 겨울에 잠을 자니?

4 They have a few (cabbages / cherries).
그들은 체리를 몇 개 가지고 있다.

5 She is (drinking / talking) to her teacher.
그녀는 그녀의 선생님에게 말하고 있다.

6 The (snake / iguana) lives in the Amazon.
그 뱀은 아마존 강에 산다.

 영어는 우리말로, 우리말은 영어로 바꿔 쓰세요.

1	mushroom	___________	2	딸	___________
3	clothes	___________	4	돼지	___________
5	hen	___________	6	오렌지	___________
7	father	___________	8	먹다	___________
9	lemon	___________	10	원숭이	___________
11	lunch	___________	12	친척	___________
13	nap	___________	14	양배추	___________
15	pet	___________	16	목욕	___________
17	duck	___________	18	기린	___________
19	grandparent	___________	20	아들	___________

F 잘 듣고, 빈칸에 알맞은 단어를 써넣어 문장을 완성하세요.

Day 10_F

1 The men pick ___________.

2 He often ___________ in the playground.

3 The ___________ are wearing the same dress.

4 Which ___________ is slower?

5 My cat ___________ on the blanket.

6 We have a ___________ tree in the yard.

7 Does your ___________ cook well?

8 The ___________ was the most colorful of the three.

G 우리말 뜻과 일치하도록 빈칸에 알맞은 단어를 써넣어 문장을 완성하세요.

1 A w_________________ is a wild animal.
늑대는 야생 동물이다.

2 My a_________________ showed me her photos.
나의 고모는 나에게 그녀의 사진들을 보여 주었다.

3 You don't have to cut a c_________________.
너는 당근을 자를 필요가 없다.

4 Did the e_________________ break the fence?
그 코끼리가 그 울타리를 부쉈니?

5 Her h_________________ is writing a letter.
그녀의 남편은 편지를 쓰고 있다.

6 You must do your h_________________ first.
너는 먼저 너의 숙제를 해야 한다.

7 Her son w_________________ his hands.
그녀의 아들은 그의 손을 씻었다.

8 My brother hates e_________________.
나의 형은 가지를 몹시 싫어한다.

9 My n_________________ is a famous singer.
나의 여자 조카는 유명한 가수이다.

10 The p_________________ costs ten dollars.
그 파인애플은 10달러이다.

✎ Review에서 틀린 문제의 영어 단어와 우리말 뜻을 쓴 다음, 영어 단어를 3번씩 쓰세요.

	(	)	_________ _________ _________
	(	)	_________ _________ _________
	(	)	_________ _________ _________
	(	)	_________ _________ _________
	(	)	_________ _________ _________

Day 11 — 식물과 곤충

01 ant
[ænt]

명 개미

Bob is touching an ant.
Bob은 개미를 만지고 있다.

02 bee
[biː]

명 벌

She is not afraid of bees.
그녀는 벌을 무서워하지 않는다.

03 bug
[bʌg]

명 벌레

Is he able to catch a bug?
그는 벌레를 잡을 수 있니?

04 bush
[buʃ]

명 덤불

His gloves were in the bush.
그의 장갑은 덤불 안에 있었다.

05 butterfly
[bʌ́tərflài]

명 나비

The butterflies have beautiful wings.
그 나비들은 아름다운 날개를 가지고 있다.

06 dragonfly
[drǽgənflài]

명 잠자리

The kids are looking for a dragonfly.
그 아이들은 잠자리를 찾고 있다.

07 flower
[fláuər]

명 꽃

I want to get flowers for my birthday gift.
나는 나의 생일 선물로 꽃을 받고 싶다.

08 fly
[flai]

명 파리

The frog caught a fly.
그 개구리는 파리 한 마리를 잡았다.

09 grass
[græs]

명 풀, 잔디

Cows usually eat grass.
소는 보통 풀을 먹는다.

10 grasshopper
[grǽshàpər]

명 메뚜기

A grasshopper can jump high.
메뚜기는 높이 점프할 수 있다.

Daily Test

A 우리말 뜻과 일치하도록 빠진 글자를 써넣어 단어를 완성하세요.

1 덤불   b __ __ __   **2** 풀, 잔디   __ r __ s __

3 개미   __ __ t   **4** 꽃   f __ __ __ e __

5 나비   __ u __ t __ __ __ __ y

B 다음 영어 단어의 우리말 뜻을 쓰세요.

1 bee   ________________   **2** dragonfly   ________________

3 grasshopper   ________________   **4** bug   ________________

5 fly   ________________

C 우리말 뜻과 일치하도록 빈칸에 알맞은 단어를 써넣어 문장을 완성하세요.

1 His gloves were in the ________________.
그의 장갑은 덤불 안에 있었다.

2 Bob is touching an ________________.
Bob은 개미를 만지고 있다.

3 The kids are looking for a ________________.
그 아이들은 잠자리를 찾고 있다.

4 Is he able to catch a ________________?
그는 벌레를 잡을 수 있니?

5 Cows usually eat ________________.
소는 보통 풀을 먹는다.

6 The frog caught a ________________.
그 개구리는 파리 한 마리를 잡았다.

7 A ________________ can jump high.
메뚜기는 높이 점프할 수 있다.

8 The ________________ have beautiful wings.
그 나비들은 아름다운 날개를 가지고 있다.

11	**insect** [ínsekt]	명 곤충 What is the name of this insect? 이 곤충의 이름은 무엇이니?
12	**ladybug** [léidibʌ̀g]	명 무당벌레 Where did they find ladybugs? 그들은 어디에서 무당벌레들을 발견했니?
13	**leaf** [liːf]	명 잎, 나뭇잎 What color are the leaves? 그 나뭇잎들은 무슨 색이니?
14	**lily** [líli]	명 백합 That lily is big and white. 저 백합은 크고 하얗다.
15	**mosquito** [məskíːtou]	명 모기 A mosquito was flying above my head. 모기 한 마리가 나의 머리 위에서 날고 있었다.
16	**plant** [plænt]	명 식물 동 심다 What are you going to plant in the garden? 너는 정원에 무엇을 심을 거니?
17	**rose** [rouz]	명 장미 They buy red, yellow, and white roses. 그들은 빨간색, 노란색, 그리고 하얀색 장미를 산다.
18	**sunflower** [sʌ́nflàuər]	명 해바라기 There are three sunflowers on the table. 탁자 위에 해바라기 세 송이가 있다.
19	**tree** [triː]	명 나무 It is climbing up the tree quickly. 그것은 그 나무를 빠르게 올라가고 있다.
20	**tulip** [tʃúːlip]	명 튤립 We can see tulips in spring. 우리는 봄에 튤립을 볼 수 있다.

A 우리말 뜻과 일치하도록 빠진 글자를 써넣어 단어를 완성하세요.

1 곤충   __ __ s __ __ t   **2** 잎, 나뭇잎   l __ __ f

3 튤립   t __ __ i __   **4** 장미   __ o __ __

5 나무   __ __ __ e

B 다음 영어 단어의 우리말 뜻을 쓰세요.

1 plant   ___________________   **2** lily   ___________________

3 ladybug   ___________________   **4** sunflower   ___________________

5 mosquito   ___________________

C 우리말 뜻과 일치하도록 빈칸에 알맞은 단어를 써넣어 문장을 완성하세요.

1 A _________________ was flying above my head.
모기 한 마리가 나의 머리 위에서 날고 있었다.

2 What color are the _________________?
그 나뭇잎들은 무슨 색이니?

3 There are three _________________ on the table.
탁자 위에 해바라기 세 송이가 있다.

4 It is climbing up the _________________ quickly.
그것은 그 나무를 빠르게 올라가고 있다.

5 That _________________ is big and white.
저 백합은 크고 하얗다.

6 What is the name of this _________________?
이 곤충의 이름은 무엇이니?

7 They buy red, yellow, and white _________________.
그들은 빨간색, 노란색, 그리고 하얀색 장미를 산다.

8 What are you going to _________________ in the garden?
너는 정원에 무엇을 심을 거니?

Day 12_01

01 chilly
[tʃíli]
형 쌀쌀한
It is pretty chilly outside.
바깥은 꽤 쌀쌀하다.

02 clear
[kliər]
형 맑은
It will be clear this Friday.
이번 주 금요일에는 맑을 것이다.

03 cloud
[klaud]
명 구름
The cloud covered the sun.
그 구름이 해를 가렸다.

04 cloudy
[kláudi]
형 흐린, 구름이 낀
His mother likes cloudy days.
그의 어머니는 흐린 날을 좋아하신다.

05 cold
[kould]
형 추운
Was it cold this morning?
오늘 아침에 추웠니?

06 cool
[ku:l]
형 시원한
We feel cool in the forest.
우리는 숲에서 시원하게 느낀다.

07 dry
[drai]
형 마른, 건조한
It was very dry last weekend.
지난 주말에는 매우 건조했다.

08 fog
[fɔ(:)g]
명 안개
How thick the fog is!
안개가 매우 짙구나!

09 foggy
[fɔ́(:)gi]
형 안개가 낀
You should not drive on a foggy day.
너는 안개 낀 날에는 운전하지 않는 것이 좋겠다.

10 hot
[hɑt]
형 더운, 뜨거운
The girl goes swimming when it is hot.
그 소녀는 더울 때 수영을 하러 간다.

Daily Test

A 우리말 뜻과 일치하도록 빠진 글자를 써넣어 단어를 완성하세요.

1 시원한   c __ __ l   **2** 안개   f __ __

3 구름   __ l __ __ d   **4** 더운, 뜨거운   __ __ t

5 추운   __ o __ __

B 다음 영어 단어의 우리말 뜻을 쓰세요.

1 clear   __________   **2** chilly   __________

3 dry   __________   **4** cloudy   __________

5 foggy   __________

C 우리말 뜻과 일치하도록 빈칸에 알맞은 단어를 써넣어 문장을 완성하세요.

1 Was it __________ this morning?
오늘 아침에 추웠니?

2 It will be __________ this Friday.
이번 주 금요일에는 맑을 것이다.

3 We feel __________ in the forest.
우리는 숲에서 시원하게 느낀다.

4 It was very __________ last weekend.
지난 주말에는 매우 건조했다.

5 The __________ covered the sun.
그 구름이 해를 가렸다.

6 The girl goes swimming when it is __________.
그 소녀는 더울 때 수영을 하러 간다.

7 You should not drive on a __________ day.
너는 안개 긴 날에는 운전하지 않는 것이 좋겠다.

8 It is pretty __________ outside.
바깥은 꽤 쌀쌀하다.

11 rain
[rein]

명 비 동 비가 오다
It rained a lot, so the ground was slippery.
비가 많이 내려서, 땅이 미끄러웠다.

12 rainy
[réini]

형 비가 오는
Stay at home on rainy days.
비가 오는 날에는 집에 있어.

13 snow
[snou]

명 눈 동 눈이 오다
I saw some footprints in the snow.
나는 눈 위에 있는 발자국들을 보았다.

14 snowy
[snóui]

형 눈이 오는
My dog loves to go outside on a snowy day.
나의 개는 눈이 오는 날에 밖에 나가는 것을 정말 좋아한다.

15 storm
[stɔːrm]

명 폭풍, 폭풍우
A storm hit the village last week.
폭풍이 지난주에 그 마을을 강타했다.

16 stormy
[stɔ́ːrmi]

형 폭풍우가 몰아치는
Airplanes can't take off because it is stormy.
폭풍우가 치기 때문에 비행기들이 이륙할 수 없다.

17 sunny
[sʌ́ni]

형 화창한
I hope it will be sunny tomorrow.
나는 내일 화창하기를 바란다.

18 warm
[wɔːrm]

형 따뜻한
Lucy felt warm in the house.
Lucy는 집 안에서 따뜻함을 느꼈다.

19 wind
[wind]

명 바람
The wind is coming from the west.
바람이 서쪽에서 오고 있다.

20 windy
[wíndi]

형 바람이 부는
A windy day is good for flying kites.
바람이 부는 날은 연을 날리기에 좋다.

Daily Test

A 우리말 뜻과 일치하도록 빠진 글자를 써넣어 단어를 완성하세요.

1 화창한   __ u __ __ __

2 눈이 오는   s __ __ w __

3 비; 비가 오다   __ __ i __

4 바람   w __ n __

5 폭풍, 폭풍우   __ t __ __ m

B 다음 영어 단어의 우리말 뜻을 쓰세요.

1 snow   __________________

2 stormy   __________________

3 rainy   __________________

4 warm   __________________

5 windy   __________________

C 우리말 뜻과 일치하도록 빈칸에 알맞은 단어를 써넣어 문장을 완성하세요.

1 Airplanes can't take off because it is __________________.
폭풍우가 치기 때문에 비행기들이 이륙할 수 없다.

2 Lucy felt __________________ in the house.
Lucy는 집 안에서 따뜻함을 느꼈다.

3 My dog loves to go outside on a __________________ day.
나의 개는 눈이 오는 날에 밖에 나가는 것을 정말 좋아한다.

4 A __________________ hit the village last week.
폭풍이 지난주에 그 마을을 강타했다.

5 A __________________ day is good for flying kites.
바람이 부는 날은 연을 날리기에 좋다.

6 Stay at home on __________________ days.
비가 오는 날에는 집에 있어.

7 The __________________ is coming from the west.
바람이 서쪽에서 오고 있다.

8 I hope it will be __________________ tomorrow.
나는 내일 화창하기를 바란다.

01 band
[bænd]

명 밴드, 악단
I want to be a member of the band.
나는 그 밴드의 멤버가 되고 싶다.

02 cello
[tʃélou]

명 첼로
This cello is very expensive.
이 첼로는 매우 비싸다.

03 classical
[klǽsikəl]

형 (음악) 클래식의, 고전적인
It is his favorite classical music.
그것은 그가 가장 좋아하는 클래식 음악이다.

04 concert
[kánsə(ː)rt]

명 연주회, 콘서트
We are watching a concert.
우리는 연주회를 보고 있다.

05 drum
[drʌm]

명 북, 드럼
Hit your drum more slowly.
너의 북을 더 느리게 쳐.

06 flute
[fluːt]

명 플루트
Is this an article about flutes?
이것은 플루트에 관한 기사니?

07 guitar
[gitáːr]

명 기타
I took guitar lessons for two years.
나는 2년 동안 기타 수업을 들었다.

08 harp
[hɑːrp]

명 하프
She is cleaning her harp.
그녀는 그녀의 하프를 닦고 있다.

09 listen
[lísn]

동 듣다　✿ listen to ~을 듣다
I always listen to the music when I'm tired.
나는 피곤할 때 항상 그 음악을 듣는다.

10 melody
[mélədi]

명 멜로디, 선율
Do you remember the melody?
너는 그 멜로디를 기억하니?

Daily Test

A 우리말 뜻과 일치하도록 빠진 글자를 써넣어 단어를 완성하세요.

1 북, 드럼   __ __ u __

2 듣다   __ __ s __ __ n

3 밴드, 악단   __ __ __ d

4 첼로   c __ __ __ o

5 기타   __ u __ __ a __

B 다음 영어 단어의 우리말 뜻을 쓰세요.

1 melody   ________________

2 concert   ________________

3 harp   ________________

4 flute   ________________

5 classical   ________________

C 우리말 뜻과 일치하도록 빈칸에 알맞은 단어를 써넣어 문장을 완성하세요.

1 This ________________ is very expensive.
이 첼로는 매우 비싸다.

2 We are watching a ________________.
우리는 연주회를 보고 있다.

3 I want to be a member of the ________________.
나는 그 밴드의 멤버가 되고 싶다.

4 I always ________________ to the music when I'm tired.
나는 피곤할 때 항상 그 음악을 듣는다.

5 Hit your ________________ more slowly.
너의 북을 더 느리게 쳐.

6 She is cleaning her ________________.
그녀는 그녀의 하프를 닦고 있다.

7 It is his favorite ________________ music.
그것은 그가 가장 좋아하는 클래식 음악이다.

8 Do you remember the ________________?
너는 그 멜로디를 기억하니?

11　opera
[ápərə]

명 오페라
They went to the opera.
그들은 오페라를 보러 갔다.

12　orchestra
[ɔ́ːrkistrə]

명 오케스트라, 관현악단
The orchestra will visit the city.
그 오케스트라는 그 도시를 방문할 것이다.

13　piano
[piǽnou]

명 피아노
The woman is sitting in front of the piano.
그 여자는 피아노 앞에 앉아 있다.

14　play
[plei]

동 연주하다
Are you going to play music on the street?
너희는 거리에서 음악을 연주할 거니?

15　recorder
[rikɔ́ːrdər]

명 리코더
They didn't bring recorders.
그들은 리코더를 가지고 오지 않았다.

16　sing
[siŋ]

동 노래를 부르다　✿ sing-sang-sung
The kid sings the best in his class.
그 아이는 그의 반에서 노래를 가장 잘 부른다.

17　song
[sɔ(ː)ŋ]

명 노래
Does the actor know this song?
그 배우는 이 노래를 아니?

18　trumpet
[trʌ́mpit]

명 트럼펫
The trumpet has a powerful sound.
그 트럼펫은 힘 있는 소리를 가지고 있다.

19　violin
[vàiəlín]

명 바이올린
My uncle is drawing a violin.
나의 삼촌은 바이올린을 그리고 있다.

20　voice
[vɔis]

명 목소리
Did you hear Tom's beautiful voice?
너는 Tom의 아름다운 목소리를 들었니?

Daily Test

A 우리말 뜻과 일치하도록 빠진 글자를 써넣어 단어를 완성하세요.

1 리코더   r __ __ o __ __ __ __ __

2 오페라   __ __ e __ a

3 바이올린   __ i __ l __ __

4 목소리   v __ __ c __

5 노래를 부르다   __ __ __ g

B 다음 영어 단어의 우리말 뜻을 쓰세요.

1 piano   _________________

2 song   _________________

3 orchestra   _________________

4 play   _________________

5 trumpet   _________________

C 우리말 뜻과 일치하도록 빈칸에 알맞은 단어를 써넣어 문장을 완성하세요.

1 The woman is sitting in front of the _________________.
그 여자는 피아노 앞에 앉아 있다.

2 My uncle is drawing a _________________.
나의 삼촌은 바이올린을 그리고 있다.

3 Does the actor know this _________________?
그 배우는 이 노래를 아니?

4 The kid _________________ the best in his class.
그 아이는 그의 반에서 노래를 가장 잘 부른다.

5 Did you hear Tom's beautiful _________________?
너는 Tom의 아름다운 목소리를 들었니?

6 The _________________ will visit the city.
그 오케스트라는 그 도시를 방문할 것이다.

7 Are you going to _________________ music on the street?
너희는 거리에서 음악을 연주할 거니?

8 The _________________ has a powerful sound.
그 트럼펫은 힘 있는 소리를 가지고 있다.

01 bathroom
[bǽθrù(:)m]
명 욕실
The towel was in the bathroom.
그 수건은 욕실에 있었다.

02 bedroom
[bédrù(:)m]
명 침실
Her bedroom is on the second floor.
그녀의 침실은 2층에 있다.

03 bell
[bel]
명 초인종, 벨, 벨 소리
She didn't hear the bell.
그녀는 그 벨 소리를 듣지 못했다.

04 carpet
[káːrpit]
명 카펫
We should not step on the carpet.
우리는 그 카펫을 밟지 않는 것이 좋겠다.

05 curtain
[káːrtən]
명 커튼
I closed the black curtains.
나는 그 검은색 커튼들을 쳤다.

06 door
[dɔːr]
명 문
I don't know how to fix this door.
나는 이 문을 어떻게 고치는지 모른다.

07 floor
[flɔːr]
명 바닥
Everyone is reading a book on the floor.
모든 사람이 바닥에서 책을 읽고 있다.

08 garden
[gáːrdən]
명 정원
Was a deer in the garden?
정원에 사슴 한 마리가 있었니?

09 gate
[geit]
명 정문, 대문
Let's paint the gate blue.
그 대문을 파란색으로 칠하자.

10 house
[haus]
명 집
There is a tree next to my house.
나의 집 옆에 나무 한 그루가 있다.

Daily Test

A 우리말 뜻과 일치하도록 빠진 글자를 써넣어 단어를 완성하세요.

1 커튼   __ u __ t __ __ __

2 집   __ __ u s __

3 정문, 대문   __ __ t __

4 카펫   c __ __ __ e __

5 침실   __ __ __ r __ o __

B 다음 영어 단어의 우리말 뜻을 쓰세요.

1 bell   __________________

2 door   __________________

3 garden   __________________

4 floor   __________________

5 bathroom   __________________

C 우리말 뜻과 일치하도록 빈칸에 알맞은 단어를 써넣어 문장을 완성하세요.

1 Her ________________ is on the second floor.
그녀의 침실은 2층에 있다.

2 I don't know how to fix this ________________.
나는 이 문을 어떻게 고치는지 모른다.

3 Was a deer in the ________________?
정원에 사슴 한 마리가 있었니?

4 She didn't hear the ________________.
그녀는 그 벨 소리를 듣지 못했다.

5 There is a tree next to my ________________.
나의 집 옆에 나무 한 그루가 있다.

6 The towel was in the ________________.
그 수건은 욕실에 있었다.

7 Let's paint the ________________ blue.
그 대문을 파란색으로 칠하자.

8 We should not step on the ________________.
우리는 그 카펫을 밟지 않는 것이 좋겠다.

11 kitchen
[kítʃən]

몡 부엌, 주방
Clean the kitchen before she comes!
그녀가 오기 전에 부엌을 청소해!

12 living room
[lívingrù(:)m]

몡 거실
The living room is the best place to watch TV.
거실은 TV를 보기에 가장 좋은 장소이다.

13 mat
[mæt]

몡 매트, 깔개
The mat got dirty because of the mud.
그 매트는 진흙 때문에 더러워졌다.

14 oven
[ʌ́vən]

몡 오븐
Which oven is cheaper?
어느 오븐이 더 싸니?

15 refrigerator
[rifrídʒərèitər]

몡 냉장고
The refrigerator was broken again.
그 냉장고는 또 고장이 났다.

16 sofa
[sóufə]

몡 소파
Where can I put this sofa?
이 소파를 어디에 둘까요?

17 switch
[switʃ]

몡 스위치
Is this a switch for the lamp?
이것이 그 램프의 스위치이니?

18 table
[téibl]

몡 탁자
The legs of this table look so weak.
이 탁자의 다리들은 매우 약해 보인다.

19 window
[wíndou]

몡 창문
The building has lots of windows.
그 건물에는 창문이 많다.

20 yard
[jɑːrd]

몡 마당, 뜰
How about camping in the yard tonight?
오늘 밤 마당에서 캠핑을 하는 게 어때?

Daily Test

A 우리말 뜻과 일치하도록 빠진 글자를 써넣어 단어를 완성하세요.

1 소파   __ __ f __

2 매트, 깔개   __ a __

3 부엌, 주방   __ i __ __ h __ __

4 마당, 뜰   y __ __ __

5 탁자   t __ __ l __

B 다음 영어 단어의 우리말 뜻을 쓰세요.

1 living room ________________

2 oven ________________

3 refrigerator ________________

4 switch ________________

5 window ________________

C 우리말 뜻과 일치하도록 빈칸에 알맞은 단어를 써넣어 문장을 완성하세요.

1 The _____________ got dirty because of the mud.
그 매트는 진흙 때문에 더러워졌다.

2 The building has lots of _____________.
그 건물에는 창문이 많다.

3 Where can I put this _____________?
이 소파를 어디에 둘까요?

4 The _____________ was broken again.
그 냉장고는 또 고장이 났다.

5 How about camping in the _____________ tonight?
오늘 밤 마당에서 캠핑을 하는 게 어때?

6 The legs of this _____________ look so weak.
이 탁자의 다리들은 매우 약해 보인다.

7 Clean the _____________ before she comes!
그녀가 오기 전에 부엌을 청소해!

8 Which _____________ is cheaper?
어느 오븐이 더 싸니?

A 우리말 뜻에 해당하는 영어 단어를 찾아 동그라미 하세요.

잎, 나뭇잎	기타	꽃	바람	탁자
플루트	흐린, 구름이 낀	연주하다	커튼	튤립

v	l	e	a	f	z	c	w	f	g
c	l	o	u	d	y	l	i	m	u
q	d	l	l	e	l	f	n	s	i
l	t	u	l	i	p	c	d	c	t
g	x	b	t	z	r	l	m	p	a
c	a	g	f	f	l	o	w	e	r
t	c	u	r	t	a	i	n	t	r
f	l	u	t	e	j	p	l	a	y

B 우리말 뜻과 일치하도록 알맞은 단어를 골라 문장을 완성하세요.

bathroom	bug	house	violin	sunny	grasshopper

1 A ________________ can jump high.
메뚜기는 높이 점프할 수 있다.

2 My uncle is drawing a ________________.
나의 삼촌은 바이올린을 그리고 있다.

3 I hope it will be ________________ tomorrow.
나는 내일 화창하기를 바란다.

4 There is a tree next to my ________________.
나의 집 옆에 나무 한 그루가 있다.

5 The towel was in the ________________.
그 수건은 욕실에 있었다.

6 Is he able to catch a ________________?
그는 벌레를 잡을 수 있니?

C 들려 주는 영어 단어를 바르게 쓴 다음, 우리말 뜻을 써넣으세요.

Day 15_C

	영어 단어	우리말		영어 단어	우리말
1			11		
2			12		
3			13		
4			14		
5			15		
6			16		
7			17		
8			18		
9			19		
10			20		

D 우리말 뜻과 일치하도록 알맞은 단어를 골라 동그라미 하세요.

1 It will be (clear / foggy) this Friday.
이번 주 금요일에는 맑을 것이다.

2 The woman is sitting in front of the (guitar / piano).
그 여자는 피아노 앞에 앉아 있다.

3 Bob is touching an (insect / ant).
Bob은 개미를 만지고 있다.

4 Everyone is reading a book on the (floor / yard).
모든 사람이 바닥에서 책을 읽고 있다.

5 A (butterfly / mosquito) was flying above my head.
모기 한 마리가 나의 머리 위에서 날고 있었다.

6 I don't know how to fix this (carpet / door).
나는 이 문을 어떻게 고치는지 모른다.

E 영어는 우리말로, 우리말은 영어로 바꿔 쓰세요.

1	grass	___________	**2**	구름	___________
3	orchestra	___________	**4**	밴드, 악단	___________
5	rainy	___________	**6**	무당벌레	___________
7	window	___________	**8**	정문, 대문	___________
9	lily	___________	**10**	더운, 뜨거운	___________
11	living room	___________	**12**	북, 드럼	___________
13	cool	___________	**14**	잠자리	___________
15	cello	___________	**16**	리코더	___________
17	mat	___________	**18**	소파	___________
19	plant	___________	**20**	추운	___________

Day 15_F

F 잘 듣고, 빈칸에 알맞은 단어를 써넣어 문장을 완성하세요.

1 She didn't hear the ___________.

2 There are three ___________ on the table.

3 She is not afraid of ___________.

4 Do you remember the ___________?

5 Her ___________ is on the second floor.

6 The ___________ has a powerful sound.

7 Airplanes can't take off because it is ___________.

8 I always ___________ to the music when I'm tired.

Day 15

G 우리말 뜻과 일치하도록 빈칸에 알맞은 단어를 써넣어 문장을 완성하세요.

1 Lucy felt w________________ in the house.
Lucy는 집 안에서 따뜻함을 느꼈다.

2 It r________________ a lot, so the ground was slippery.
비가 많이 내려서, 땅이 미끄러웠다.

3 She is cleaning her h________________.
그녀는 그녀의 하프를 닦고 있다.

4 How thick the f________________ is!
안개가 매우 짙구나!

5 The frog caught a f________________.
그 개구리는 파리 한 마리를 잡았다.

6 My dog loves to go outside on a s________________ day.
나의 개는 눈이 오는 날에 밖에 나가는 것을 정말 좋아한다.

7 Which o________________ is cheaper?
어느 오븐이 더 싸니?

8 A w________________ day is good for flying kites.
바람이 부는 날은 연을 날리기에 좋다.

9 The r________________ was broken again.
그 냉장고는 또 고장이 났다.

10 Does the actor know this s________________?
그 배우는 이 노래를 아니?

Review에서 틀린 문제의 영어 단어와 우리말 뜻을 쓴 다음, 영어 단어를 3번씩 쓰세요.

01 boots
[buːts]

명 부츠, 장화
The soldiers always wear boots.
그 군인들은 항상 부츠를 신는다.

02 button
[bʌ́tən]

명 단추, 버튼
I keep these buttons in my drawer.
나는 이 단추들을 나의 서랍에 보관한다.

03 cap
[kæp]

명 (앞에 챙이 달린) 모자
I'd like to exchange this cap.
나는 이 모자를 교환하고 싶다.

04 coat
[kout]

명 외투, 코트
Put on the thick coat.
그 두꺼운 코트를 입어.

05 dress
[dres]

명 원피스, 드레스
The white dress is for a special day.
그 하얀 드레스는 특별한 날을 위한 것이다.

06 gloves
[glʌvz]

명 장갑
My gloves got wet in the rain.
나의 장갑이 비에 젖었다.

07 hat
[hæt]

명 모자
The hat is a gift from Dad.
그 모자는 아빠가 주신 선물이다.

08 jeans
[dʒiːnz]

명 청바지
The jeans are $320.
그 청바지는 320달러이다.

09 pants
[pænts]

명 바지
Will you bring me those pants?
저 바지를 나에게 가져다 줄래?

10 pocket
[pákit]

명 주머니
What is in your pocket?
너의 주머니에 무엇이 있니?

Daily Test

A 우리말 뜻과 일치하도록 빠진 글자를 써넣어 단어를 완성하세요.

1 단추, 버튼 __ u __ __ o __

2 원피스, 드레스 __ __ __ s __

3 주머니 __ o __ k __ __

4 부츠, 장화 b __ __ __ s

5 모자 h __ __

B 다음 영어 단어의 우리말 뜻을 쓰세요.

1 pants ___________________

2 gloves ___________________

3 jeans ___________________

4 coat ___________________

5 cap ___________________

C 우리말 뜻과 일치하도록 빈칸에 알맞은 단어를 써넣어 문장을 완성하세요.

1 I keep these _______________ in my drawer.
나는 이 단추들을 나의 서랍에 보관한다.

2 The soldiers always wear _______________.
그 군인들은 항상 부츠를 신는다.

3 The _______________ are $320.
그 청바지는 320달러이다.

4 My _______________ got wet in the rain.
나의 장갑이 비에 젖었다.

5 The white _______________ is for a special day.
그 하얀 드레스는 특별한 날을 위한 것이다.

6 Will you bring me those _______________?
저 바지를 나에게 가져다 줄래?

7 Put on the thick _______________.
그 두꺼운 코트를 입어.

8 What is in your _______________?
너의 주머니에 무엇이 있니?

11 ribbon
[ríbən]

명 리본
The ribbon is not mine.
그 리본은 나의 것이 아니다.

12 shirt
[ʃəːrt]

명 셔츠
Did she buy any shirts?
그녀는 셔츠를 샀니?

13 shoes
[ʃuːz]

명 신발
They sold their shoes at the flea market.
그들은 벼룩시장에서 그들의 신발을 팔았다.

14 shorts
[ʃɔːrts]

명 반바지
We must not wear shorts there.
우리는 거기에서 반바지를 입으면 안 된다.

15 skirt
[skəːrt]

명 치마
Do you like a long skirt?
너는 긴 치마를 좋아하니?

16 sneakers
[sníkərz]

명 운동화
Kathy washes her sneakers by herself.
Kathy는 그녀의 운동화를 스스로 빤다.

17 socks
[saks]

명 양말
I took off my socks.
나는 나의 양말을 벗었다.

18 sweater
[swétər]

명 스웨터
Whom are you knitting the sweater for?
너는 누구를 위해 그 스웨터를 뜨고 있니?

19 tie
[tai]

명 넥타이
His tie is too long.
그의 넥타이는 너무 길다.

20 T-shirt
[tíːʃəːrt]

명 티셔츠
That T-shirt looks good on you.
저 티셔츠는 너에게 잘 어울린다.

Daily Test

A 우리말 뜻과 일치하도록 빠진 글자를 써넣어 단어를 완성하세요.

1 넥타이　　　t＿＿

2 반바지　　　＿＿＿r＿s

3 스웨터　　　＿w＿＿t＿r

4 리본　　　　＿＿b＿o＿

5 치마　　　　s＿＿r＿

B 다음 영어 단어의 우리말 뜻을 쓰세요.

1 T-shirt　　　＿＿＿＿＿＿＿＿

2 sneakers　　＿＿＿＿＿＿＿＿

3 shirt　　　　＿＿＿＿＿＿＿＿

4 socks　　　　＿＿＿＿＿＿＿＿

5 shoes　　　　＿＿＿＿＿＿＿＿

C 우리말 뜻과 일치하도록 빈칸에 알맞은 단어를 써넣어 문장을 완성하세요.

1 Kathy washes her ＿＿＿＿＿＿＿＿ by herself.
　Kathy는 그녀의 운동화를 스스로 빤다.

2 Whom are you knitting the ＿＿＿＿＿＿＿＿ for?
　너는 누구를 위해 그 스웨터를 뜨고 있니?

3 The ＿＿＿＿＿＿＿＿ is not mine.
　그 리본은 나의 것이 아니다.

4 Do you like a long ＿＿＿＿＿＿＿＿?
　너는 긴 치마를 좋아하니?

5 That ＿＿＿＿＿＿＿＿ looks good on you.
　저 티셔츠는 너에게 잘 어울린다.

6 I took off my ＿＿＿＿＿＿＿＿.
　나는 나의 양말을 벗었다.

7 We must not wear ＿＿＿＿＿＿＿＿ there.
　우리는 거기에서 반바지를 입으면 안 된다.

8 His ＿＿＿＿＿＿＿＿ is too long.
　그의 넥타이는 너무 길다.

01 badminton
[bǽdmintən]

명 배드민턴
Badminton is a popular sport.
배드민턴은 인기 있는 스포츠이다.

02 baseball
[béisbɔ̀ːl]

명 야구, 야구공
I enjoy watching a baseball game.
나는 야구 경기를 보는 것을 즐긴다.

03 basketball
[bǽskitbɔ̀ːl]

명 농구, 농구공
My friend is a big fan of basketball.
나의 친구는 엄청난 농구 팬이다.

04 boxing
[báksiŋ]

명 권투, 복싱
Jake does boxing every Sunday.
Jake는 매주 일요일에 권투를 한다.

05 coach
[koutʃ]

명 코치
The coach is choosing a ball.
그 코치는 공을 고르고 있다.

06 court
[kɔːrt]

명 (테니스 등의) 코트
This court is small and dirty.
이 코트는 작고 더럽다.

07 fencing
[fénsiŋ]

명 펜싱
Fencing is exciting, isn't it?
펜싱은 신나, 그렇지 않니?

08 golf
[gɑlf]

명 골프
Why is the boy learning golf?
그 소년은 왜 골프를 배우고 있니?

09 jog
[dʒɑg]

동 조깅하다
He jogs one kilometer every day.
그는 매일 1킬로미터를 조깅한다.

10 medal
[médəl]

명 메달
He could not win the gold medal.
그는 금메달을 따지 못했다.

Daily Test

A 우리말 뜻과 일치하도록 빠진 글자를 써넣어 단어를 완성하세요.

1 펜싱 f _ _ c _ _ g

2 권투, 복싱 _ _ x _ _ g

3 코치 c _ _ _ h

4 조깅하다 _ o _

5 야구, 야구공 _ a _ _ _ a _ _

B 다음 영어 단어의 우리말 뜻을 쓰세요.

1 badminton ___________________

2 medal ___________________

3 golf ___________________

4 court ___________________

5 basketball ___________________

C 우리말 뜻과 일치하도록 빈칸에 알맞은 단어를 써넣어 문장을 완성하세요.

1 The ___________________ is choosing a ball.
그 코치는 공을 고르고 있다.

2 Jake does ___________________ every Sunday.
Jake는 매주 일요일에 권투를 한다.

3 He could not win the gold ___________________.
그는 금메달을 따지 못했다.

4 ___________________ is a popular sport.
배드민턴은 인기 있는 스포츠이다.

5 ___________________ is exciting, isn't it?
펜싱은 신나, 그렇지 않니?

6 I enjoy watching a ___________________ game.
나는 야구 경기를 보는 것을 즐긴다.

7 He ___________________ one kilometer every day.
그는 매일 1킬로미터를 조깅한다.

8 Why is the boy learning ___________________?
그 소년은 왜 골프를 배우고 있니?

11 player
[pléiər]

명 선수
She tries to be a good player.
그녀는 좋은 선수가 되기 위해 노력한다.

12 racket
[rǽkit]

명 라켓
The rackets are on sale now.
그 라켓들은 지금 세일 중이다.

13 run
[rʌn]

동 달리다　✿ run-ran-run
Be careful when you run outside.
밖에서 달릴 때는 조심해.

14 score
[skɔːr]

명 득점, 점수
What's the score now?
지금 점수가 어떻게 되니?

15 skating
[skéitiŋ]

명 스케이팅, 스케이트 (타기)
Winter is the best season for skating.
겨울은 스케이트를 타기에 가장 좋은 계절이다.

16 skiing
[skíːiŋ]

명 스키 (타기)
Did you warm up before skiing?
너는 스키를 타기 전에 준비 운동을 했니?

17 soccer
[sákər]

명 축구
They have four tickets for the soccer game.
그들은 그 축구 경기의 입장권을 4장 가지고 있다.

18 swimming
[swímiŋ]

명 수영
Don't skip the swimming lesson today.
오늘 수영 수업을 빼먹지 마.

19 team
[tiːm]

명 팀
The new team won the final game.
그 새로운 팀이 결승전에서 이겼다.

20 tennis
[ténis]

명 테니스
Tennis first started in Europe.
테니스는 유럽에서 처음 시작되었다.

A 우리말 뜻과 일치하도록 빠진 글자를 써넣어 단어를 완성하세요.

1 라켓   __ __ c __ e __   2 득점, 점수   s __ __ r __

3 팀   t __ __ __   4 선수   __ l __ __ e __

5 축구   __ o __ c __ __

B 다음 영어 단어의 우리말 뜻을 쓰세요.

1 swimming   __________   2 run   __________

3 skiing   __________   4 skating   __________

5 tennis   __________

C 우리말 뜻과 일치하도록 빈칸에 알맞은 단어를 써넣어 문장을 완성하세요.

1 She tries to be a good __________.
그녀는 좋은 선수가 되기 위해 노력한다.

2 They have four tickets for the __________ game.
그들은 그 축구 경기의 입장권을 4장 가지고 있다.

3 What's the __________ now?
지금 점수가 어떻게 되니?

4 Be careful when you __________ outside.
밖에서 달릴 때는 조심해.

5 Don't skip the __________ lesson today.
오늘 수영 수업을 빼먹지 마.

6 The new __________ won the final game.
그 새로운 팀이 결승전에서 이겼다.

7 __________ first started in Europe.
테니스는 유럽에서 처음 시작되었다.

8 The __________ are on sale now.
그 라켓들은 지금 세일 중이다.

01 alike [əláik]
형 비슷한　부 비슷하게
The boys look very alike.
그 소년들은 매우 비슷하게 생겼다.

02 chin [tʃin]
명 턱
Lift your chin and look at the sky.
턱을 들고 하늘을 봐.

03 curly [kə́ːrli]
형 곱슬곱슬한
My uncle has curly hair.
나의 삼촌은 곱슬곱슬한 머리를 가지고 있다.

04 cute [kjuːt]
형 귀여운
She is playing with her cute sister.
그녀는 그녀의 귀여운 여동생과 놀고 있다.

05 ear [iər]
명 귀
Her daughter has big ears.
그녀의 딸은 큰 귀를 가지고 있다.

06 eye [ai]
명 눈
My right eye is bigger than my left eye.
나의 오른쪽 눈은 나의 왼쪽 눈보다 더 크다.

07 face [feis]
명 얼굴
Wash your face and body now!
지금 너의 얼굴과 몸을 씻어!

08 fat [fæt]
형 뚱뚱한
The doctor is fat, isn't he?
그 의사는 뚱뚱해, 그렇지 않니?

09 hair [hɛər]
명 머리카락, 털
I want to brush my hair.
나는 나의 머리를 빗고 싶다.

10 handsome [hǽnsəm]
형 잘생긴
He is a handsome actor.
그는 잘생긴 배우이다.

Daily Test

A 우리말 뜻과 일치하도록 빠진 글자를 써넣어 단어를 완성하세요.

1 머리카락, 털   __ a __ __

2 귀   e __ __

3 턱   __ __ i __

4 뚱뚱한   __ __ t

5 잘생긴   __ __ n __ s __ __ __

B 다음 영어 단어의 우리말 뜻을 쓰세요.

1 alike   ___________________

2 face   ___________________

3 eye   ___________________

4 cute   ___________________

5 curly   ___________________

C 우리말 뜻과 일치하도록 빈칸에 알맞은 단어를 써넣어 문장을 완성하세요.

1 The doctor is _________________, isn't he?
그 의사는 뚱뚱해, 그렇지 않니?

2 The boys look very _______________.
그 소년들은 매우 비슷하게 생겼다.

3 My right _______________ is bigger than my left _______________.
나의 오른쪽 눈은 나의 왼쪽 눈보다 더 크다.

4 He is a _______________ actor.
그는 잘생긴 배우이다.

5 Lift your _______________ and look at the sky.
턱을 들고 하늘을 봐.

6 Wash your _______________ and body now!
지금 너의 얼굴과 몸을 씻어!

7 She is playing with her _______________ sister.
그녀는 그녀의 귀여운 여동생과 놀고 있다.

8 I want to brush my _______________.
나는 나의 머리를 빗고 싶다.

11 lovely
[lʌ́vli]

웹 사랑스러운
The baby is really lovely.
그 아기는 정말 사랑스럽다.

12 mouth
[mauθ]

명 입
He opened his mouth to eat a hamburger.
그는 햄버거를 먹기 위해 그의 입을 벌렸다.

13 nose
[nouz]

명 코
A fly sat on Amy's nose.
파리가 Amy의 코에 앉았다.

14 pretty
[príti]

형 예쁜
She looks so pretty in the dress.
그녀는 그 드레스를 입으니 매우 예뻐 보인다.

15 short
[ʃɔːrt]

형 키가 작은
That short boy is my brother.
저 키가 작은 소년은 나의 남동생이다.

16 skin
[skin]

명 피부
This cream is for dry skin.
이 크림은 건조한 피부용이다.

17 slim
[slim]

형 날씬한
He tries hard to stay slim.
그는 날씬한 몸매를 유지하려고 열심히 노력한다.

18 tall
[tɔːl]

형 키가 큰
The girl is the tallest in the school.
그 소녀는 그 학교에서 가장 키가 크다.

19 tooth
[tuːθ]

명 치아, 이빨   ✿ 복수형 teeth
The dentist will pull out my tooth today.
그 치과 의사는 오늘 나의 이를 뽑을 것이다.

20 ugly
[ʌ́gli]

형 못생긴, 보기 싫은
The witch in the movie is ugly.
그 영화에 나오는 마녀는 못생겼다.

Daily Test

A 우리말 뜻과 일치하도록 빠진 글자를 써넣어 단어를 완성하세요.

1 날씬한   __ l __ __   **2** 입   __ o u __ __

3 못생긴, 보기 싫은   u __ __ __   **4** 코   n __ __ __

5 키가 큰   __ __ l __

B 다음 영어 단어의 우리말 뜻을 쓰세요.

1 pretty __________________   **2** short __________________

3 tooth __________________   **4** lovely __________________

5 skin __________________

C 우리말 뜻과 일치하도록 빈칸에 알맞은 단어를 써넣어 문장을 완성하세요.

1 She looks so _________________ in the dress.
그녀는 그 드레스를 입으니 매우 예뻐 보인다.

2 He opened his _________________ to eat a hamburger.
그는 햄버거를 먹기 위해 그의 입을 벌렸다.

3 This cream is for dry _________________.
이 크림은 건조한 피부용이다.

4 The baby is really _________________.
그 아기는 정말 사랑스럽다.

5 The witch in the movie is _________________.
그 영화에 나오는 마녀는 못생겼다.

6 He tries hard to stay _________________.
그는 날씬한 몸매를 유지하려고 열심히 노력한다.

7 The dentist will pull out my _________________ today.
그 치과 의사는 오늘 나의 이를 뽑을 것이다.

8 A fly sat on Amy's _________________.
파리가 Amy의 코에 앉았다.

01 afraid
[əfréid]

형 두려워하는
We don't have to be afraid of the shark.
우리는 그 상어를 두려워할 필요가 없다.

02 angry
[æŋgri]

형 화가 난
He will be angry if you are late.
네가 늦으면, 그는 화를 낼 것이다.

03 bad
[bæd]

형 안 좋은, 나쁜
Did the news make her feel bad?
그 소식이 그녀를 기분 나쁘게 만들었니?

04 bored
[bɔːrd]

형 지루해하는
The people were bored with the movie.
그 사람들은 그 영화를 지루해했다.

05 cry
[krai]

동 울다
The baby started to cry.
그 아기는 울기 시작했다.

06 excited
[iksáitid]

형 신이 난, 흥분한
Paul is excited about the picnic.
Paul은 소풍 때문에 신이 나 있다.

07 fear
[fiər]

명 두려움, 공포
Some people have a fear of ghosts.
어떤 사람들은 유령에 대한 두려움을 가지고 있다.

08 feeling
[fíːliŋ]

명 감정, 느낌, 기분
She doesn't express her feelings.
그녀는 그녀의 감정을 표현하지 않는다.

09 fun
[fʌn]

명 재미 형 재미있는
The party was a lot of fun.
그 파티는 정말 재미있었다.

10 glad
[glæd]

형 기쁜, 반가운
I'm glad to meet you.
만나서 반가워요.

Daily Test

A 우리말 뜻과 일치하도록 빠진 글자를 써넣어 단어를 완성하세요.

1 화가 난   __ __ g __ y   **2** 두려움, 공포   f __ __ r

3 안 좋은, 나쁜   __ __ d   **4** 재미; 재미있는   __ u __

5 기쁜, 반가운   g __ a __

B 다음 영어 단어의 우리말 뜻을 쓰세요.

1 feeling   __________________   **2** bored   __________________

3 cry   __________________   **4** excited   __________________

5 afraid   __________________

C 우리말 뜻과 일치하도록 빈칸에 알맞은 단어를 써넣어 문장을 완성하세요.

1 The baby started to _________________.
그 아기는 울기 시작했다.

2 He will be _________________ if you are late.
네가 늦으면, 그는 화를 낼 것이다.

3 Paul is _________________ about the picnic.
Paul은 소풍 때문에 신이 나 있다.

4 The people were _________________ with the movie.
그 사람들은 그 영화를 지루해했다.

5 We don't have to be _________________ of the shark.
우리는 그 상어를 두려워할 필요가 없다.

6 The party was a lot of _________________.
그 파티는 정말 재미있었다.

7 Some people have a _________________ of ghosts.
어떤 사람들은 유령에 대한 두려움을 가지고 있다.

8 Did the news make her feel _________________?
그 소식이 그녀를 기분 나쁘게 만들었니?

11 happy
[hǽpi]

형 행복한, 만족스러운
I had a happy childhood.
나는 행복한 어린 시절을 보냈다.

12 hate
[heit]

동 몹시 싫어하다, 미워하다
They hate running.
그들은 달리는 것을 몹시 싫어한다.

13 interested
[íntərəstəd]

형 흥미가 있는, 관심이 있는
Ann is very interested in science.
Ann은 과학에 매우 관심이 있다.

14 joy
[dʒɔi]

명 기쁨, 환희
Her brother danced with joy.
그녀의 남동생은 기뻐서 춤을 추었다.

15 laugh
[læf]

동 웃다
The girl was laughing loudly.
그 소녀는 큰 소리로 웃고 있었다.

16 mad
[mæd]

형 몹시 화가 난, 미친
The woman was mad because he lied.
그가 거짓말을 했기 때문에 그 여자는 몹시 화가 났다.

17 nervous
[nə́ːrvəs]

형 초조해하는
Breathe deeply when you're nervous.
초조할 때는 숨을 깊게 쉬어.

18 sad
[sæd]

형 슬픈
Everyone felt sad about his death.
모든 사람이 그의 죽음에 대해 슬퍼했다.

19 sorry
[sɔ́(ː)ri]

형 유감스러운, 미안한
I'm sorry to hear that.
참 안됐군요. / 그 소식을 듣게 되어 유감입니다.

20 want
[wɑnt]

동 원하다
All the children want milk.
그 모든 어린이들은 우유를 원한다.

Daily Test

A 우리말 뜻과 일치하도록 빠진 글자를 써넣어 단어를 완성하세요.

1 웃다 l __ u __ __

2 기쁨, 환희 __ __ y

3 유감스러운, 미안한 __ o __ r __

4 슬픈 s __ __

5 흥미가 있는 i __ t __ __ __ __ t __ __

B 다음 영어 단어의 우리말 뜻을 쓰세요.

1 want _________________

2 happy _________________

3 nervous _________________

4 mad _________________

5 hate _________________

C 우리말 뜻과 일치하도록 빈칸에 알맞은 단어를 써넣어 문장을 완성하세요.

1 The girl was _______________ loudly.
그 소녀는 큰 소리로 웃고 있었다.

2 Everyone felt _______________ about his death.
모든 사람이 그의 죽음에 대해 슬퍼했다.

3 They _______________ running.
그들은 달리는 것을 몹시 싫어한다.

4 I had a _______________ childhood.
나는 행복한 어린 시절을 보냈다.

5 Breathe deeply when you're _______________.
초조할 때는 숨을 깊게 쉬어.

6 All the children _______________ milk.
그 모든 어린이들은 우유를 원한다.

7 Ann is very _______________ in science.
Ann은 과학에 매우 관심이 있다.

8 The woman was _______________ because he lied.
그가 거짓말을 했기 때문에 그 여자는 몹시 화가 났다.

A 우리말 뜻에 해당하는 영어 단어를 찾아 동그라미 하세요.

| 수영 | 웃다 | 조깅하다 | 셔츠 | 팀 |
| 귀여운 | 단추, 버튼 | 날씬한 | 울다 | 외투, 코트 |

b	u	t	t	o	n	g	f	k	s
b	j	s	w	i	m	m	i	n	g
v	o	y	d	f	h	w	z	w	h
x	g	s	h	i	r	t	n	h	s
c	u	t	e	g	s	r	g	g	l
r	h	z	k	w	w	u	j	s	i
y	j	d	r	q	a	t	e	a	m
c	b	y	s	l	d	c	o	a	t

B 우리말 뜻과 일치하도록 알맞은 단어를 골라 문장을 완성하세요.

| shoes | nose | gloves | fear | happy | baseball |

1 My ________________ got wet in the rain.
나의 장갑이 비에 젖었다.

2 Some people have a ________________ of ghosts.
어떤 사람들은 유령에 대한 두려움을 가지고 있다.

3 A fly sat on Amy's ________________.
파리가 Amy의 코에 앉았다.

4 I had a ________________ childhood.
나는 행복한 어린 시절을 보냈다.

5 I enjoy watching a ________________ game.
나는 야구 경기를 보는 것을 즐긴다.

6 They sold their ________________ at the flea market.
그들은 벼룩시장에서 그들의 신발을 팔았다.

C 들려 주는 영어 단어를 바르게 쓴 다음, 우리말 뜻을 써넣으세요.

Day 20_C

	영어 단어	우리말		영어 단어	우리말
1			11		
2			12		
3			13		
4			14		
5			15		
6			16		
7			17		
8			18		
9			19		
10			20		

D 우리말 뜻과 일치하도록 알맞은 단어를 골라 동그라미 하세요.

1 He could not win the gold (medal / gym).
그는 금메달을 따지 못했다.

2 That (short / slim) boy is my brother.
저 키가 작은 소년은 나의 남동생이다.

3 The dentist will pull out my (tooth / nose) today.
그 치과 의사는 오늘 나의 이를 뽑을 것이다.

4 Whom are you knitting the (pants / sweater) for?
너는 누구를 위해 그 스웨터를 뜨고 있니?

5 Breathe deeply when you're (bad / nervous).
초조할 때는 숨을 깊게 쉬어.

6 They (want / hate) running.
그들은 달리는 것을 몹시 싫어한다.

1 boots ___________________ 2 잘생긴 ___________________

3 eye ___________________ 4 청바지 ___________________

5 golf ___________________ 6 원하다 ___________________

7 curly ___________________ 8 코치 ___________________

9 socks ___________________ 10 흥미가 있는 ___________________

11 hair ___________________ 12 스키 (타기) ___________________

13 mad ___________________ 14 키가 큰 ___________________

15 skating ___________________ 16 반바지 ___________________

17 bored ___________________ 18 두려워하는 ___________________

19 pocket ___________________ 20 선수 ___________________

F 잘 듣고, 빈칸에 알맞은 단어를 써넣어 문장을 완성하세요.

Day 20_F

1 The party was a lot of ___________________.

2 His ___________________ is too long.

3 What's the ___________________ now?

4 Kathy washes her ___________________ by herself.

5 This ___________________ is small and dirty.

6 Her daughter has big ___________________.

7 Lift your ___________________ and look at the sky.

8 I'd like to exchange this ___________________.

G 우리말 뜻과 일치하도록 빈칸에 알맞은 단어를 써넣어 문장을 완성하세요.

1 Paul is e________________ about the picnic.
   Paul은 소풍 때문에 신이 나 있다.

2 The white d________________ is for a special day.
   그 하얀 드레스는 특별한 날을 위한 것이다.

3 My friend is a big fan of b________________.
   나의 친구는 엄청난 농구 팬이다.

4 He will be a________________ if you are late.
   네가 늦으면, 그는 화를 낼 것이다.

5 They have four tickets for the s________________ game.
   그들은 그 축구 경기의 입장권을 4장 가지고 있다.

6 Everyone felt s________________ about his death.
   모든 사람이 그의 죽음에 대해 슬퍼했다.

7 He opened his m________________ to eat a hamburger.
   그는 햄버거를 먹기 위해 그의 입을 벌렸다.

8 The r________________ are on sale now.
   그 라켓들은 지금 세일 중이다.

9 The doctor is f________________, isn't he?
   그 의사는 뚱뚱해, 그렇지 않니?

10 She looks so p________________ in the dress.
   그녀는 그 드레스를 입으니 매우 예뻐 보인다.

Review에서 틀린 문제의 영어 단어와 우리말 뜻을 쓴 다음, 영어 단어를 3번씩 쓰세요.

	( )	________ ________ ________
	( )	________ ________ ________
	( )	________ ________ ________
	( )	________ ________ ________
	( )	________ ________ ________

01	**bitter** [bítər]	형 맛이 쓴 They shared the bitter chocolate. 그들은 그 쓴 초콜릿을 나눠 먹었다.
02	**delicious** [dilíʃəs]	형 맛있는 The steak was really delicious. 그 스테이크는 정말 맛있었다.
03	**feel** [fiːl]	동 느끼다 ✿ feel-felt-felt I felt the cold wind. 나는 차가운 바람을 느꼈다.
04	**flavor** [fléivər]	명 맛 This cream has an orange flavor. 이 크림은 오렌지 맛이 난다.
05	**fresh** [freʃ]	형 신선한 You can buy fresh tomatoes on the farm. 너희는 그 농장에서 신선한 토마토를 살 수 있다.
06	**hear** [hiər]	동 듣다 ✿ hear-heard-heard Bill heard a strange voice. Bill은 이상한 목소리를 들었다.
07	**look** [luk]	동 ~해 보이다 You look nice today. 너는 오늘 멋져 보인다.
08	**loud** [laud]	형 소리가 큰 The radio was too loud. 라디오 소리가 너무 컸다.
09	**noise** [nɔiz]	명 소음 What's that noise in the hall? 복도에서 나는 저 소음은 뭐지?
10	**salty** [sɔ́ːlti]	형 맛이 짠 The soup was salty, so I drank water. 그 수프가 짜서, 나는 물을 마셨다.

Daily Test

A 우리말 뜻과 일치하도록 빠진 글자를 써넣어 단어를 완성하세요.

1 신선한　　　　f __ __ s __

2 소리가 큰　　　　l __ u __

3 소음　　　　__ o __ s __

4 느끼다　　　　__ __ __ l

5 맛있는　　　　__ __ l __ c i __ __ __

B 다음 영어 단어의 우리말 뜻을 쓰세요.

1 look　　　________________

2 flavor　　　________________

3 salty　　　________________

4 hear　　　________________

5 bitter　　　________________

C 우리말 뜻과 일치하도록 빈칸에 알맞은 단어를 써넣어 문장을 완성하세요.

1 Bill ________________ a strange voice.
Bill은 이상한 목소리를 들었다.

2 I ________________ the cold wind.
나는 차가운 바람을 느꼈다.

3 The radio was too ________________.
라디오 소리가 너무 컸다.

4 The steak was really ________________.
그 스테이크는 정말 맛있었다.

5 The soup was ________________, so I drank water.
그 수프가 짜서, 나는 물을 마셨다.

6 What's that ________________ in the hall?
복도에서 나는 저 소음은 뭐지?

7 You can buy ________________ tomatoes on the farm.
너희는 그 농장에서 신선한 토마토를 살 수 있다.

8 You ________________ nice today.
너는 오늘 멋져 보인다.

Day 21_02

11 see
[si:]
동 보다 ✿ see-saw-seen
We can see many clouds now.
우리는 지금 많은 구름을 볼 수 있다.

12 sense
[sens]
명 감각
We have five senses.
우리는 오감을 가지고 있다.

13 smell
[smel]
동 ~ 냄새가 나다   명 냄새
Where does the smell come from?
그 냄새는 어디에서 오니?

14 sniff
[snif]
동 (코를 킁킁거리며) 냄새를 맡다
The dog was sniffing at the box.
그 개는 그 상자의 냄새를 맡고 있었다.

15 sound
[saund]
명 소리
There was no sound in the house.
그 집에서는 아무 소리도 나지 않았다.

16 sour
[sauər]
형 맛이 신
These lemons are not sour.
이 레몬들은 시지 않다.

17 spicy
[spáisi]
형 매운, 맛이 강한
He can eat spicy food very well.
그는 매운 음식을 매우 잘 먹을 수 있다.

18 sweet
[swi:t]
형 달콤한
Sweet food makes me happy.
달콤한 음식은 나를 행복하게 한다.

19 taste
[teist]
명 맛   동 ~ 맛이 나다
This pumpkin pie tastes good.
이 호박 파이는 맛이 좋다.

20 touch
[tʌtʃ]
동 만지다
Be careful when you touch the kitten.
그 새끼 고양이를 만질 때는 조심해.

Daily Test

 우리말 뜻과 일치하도록 빠진 글자를 써넣어 단어를 완성하세요.

1 감각   s _ n _ _

2 달콤한   _ _ e _ t

3 만지다   _ _ u _ h

4 맛이 신   _ _ _ r

5 보다   _ _ e

B 다음 영어 단어의 우리말 뜻을 쓰세요.

1 smell _________________

2 taste _________________

3 sound _________________

4 sniff _________________

5 spicy _________________

C 우리말 뜻과 일치하도록 빈칸에 알맞은 단어를 써넣어 문장을 완성하세요.

1 The dog was _________________ at the box.
그 개는 그 상자의 냄새를 맡고 있었다.

2 He can eat _________________ food very well.
그는 매운 음식을 매우 잘 먹을 수 있다.

3 We can _________________ many clouds now.
우리는 지금 많은 구름을 볼 수 있다.

4 We have five _________________.
우리는 오감을 가지고 있다.

5 _________________ food makes me happy.
달콤한 음식은 나를 행복하게 한다.

6 These lemons are not _________________.
이 레몬들은 시지 않다.

7 Be careful when you _________________ the kitten.
그 새끼 고양이를 만질 때는 조심해.

8 Where does the _________________ come from?
그 냄새는 어디에서 오니?

01	**bend** [bend]	동 굽히다, 구부리다 ✿ bend-bent-bent **Bend** your knees slowly. 너의 무릎을 천천히 구부려.
02	**bite** [bait]	동 (이로) 물다 ✿ bite-bit-bitten The puppy **bit** my pants. 그 강아지는 나의 바지를 물었다.
03	**bounce** [bauns]	동 튀다, 튀기다 The boy **bounced** the big ball. 그 소년은 그 큰 공을 튀겼다.
04	**catch** [kætʃ]	동 잡다 ✿ catch-caught-caught She is trying to **catch** the kite. 그녀는 그 연을 잡으려고 애쓰고 있다.
05	**chew** [tʃuː]	동 씹다 We should **chew** our food well. 우리는 음식을 잘 씹어야 한다.
06	**clap** [klæp]	동 박수를 치다 They **clapped** after the show. 그들은 쇼가 끝난 후에 박수를 쳤다.
07	**crawl** [krɔːl]	동 기다 The baby finally began to **crawl**. 그 아기는 마침내 기기 시작했다.
08	**dive** [daiv]	동 다이빙하다 My friends **dived** into the water. 나의 친구들은 물속으로 다이빙했다.
09	**float** [flout]	동 (물 위나 공중에서) 떠가다 The huge ship will **float** on water. 그 거대한 배는 물에 뜰 것이다.
10	**fly** [flai]	동 날다, 날리다 ✿ fly-flew-flown The birds are **flying** between the houses. 그 새들은 집들 사이로 날고 있다.

Daily Test

A 우리말 뜻과 일치하도록 빠진 글자를 써넣어 단어를 완성하세요.

1 씹다   __ __ __ w   **2** 날다, 날리다   f __ __

3 (이로) 물다   __ __ t __   **4** 잡다   __ __ t __ h

5 다이빙하다   __ __ __ e

B 다음 영어 단어의 우리말 뜻을 쓰세요.

1 crawl _________________   **2** clap _________________

3 bounce _________________   **4** float _________________

5 bend _________________

C 우리말 뜻과 일치하도록 빈칸에 알맞은 단어를 써넣어 문장을 완성하세요.

1 We should _________________ our food well.
우리는 음식을 잘 씹어야 한다.

2 My friends _________________ into the water.
나의 친구들은 물속으로 다이빙했다.

3 They _________________ after the show.
그들은 쇼가 끝난 후에 박수를 쳤다.

4 The boy _________________ the big ball.
그 소년은 그 큰 공을 튀겼다.

5 _________________ your knees slowly.
너의 무릎을 천천히 구부려.

6 The birds are _________________ between the houses.
그 새들은 집들 사이로 날고 있다.

7 She is trying to _________________ the kite.
그녀는 그 연을 잡으려고 애쓰고 있다.

8 The baby finally began to _________________ .
그 아기는 마침내 기기 시작했다.

11	**hang** [hæŋ]	동 걸다, 매달다 ✿ hang-hung-hung I can't **hang** my shirt in the closet. 나는 옷장에 나의 셔츠를 걸 수 없다.
12	**hit** [hit]	동 때리다, 치다 ✿ hit-hit-hit Kathy **hit** the box with a stick. Kathy는 막대기로 그 상자를 쳤다.
13	**hold** [hould]	동 잡고 있다, 들고 있다 ✿ hold-held-held They were **holding** hands. 그들은 손을 잡고 있었다.
14	**hop** [hɑp]	동 한 발로 깡충깡충 뛰다 A little girl is **hopping** in the park. 작은 소녀가 공원에서 한 발로 깡충깡충 뛰고 있다.
15	**jump** [dʒʌmp]	동 점프하다 Stop **jumping** on the bed! 침대에서 점프하는 것을 멈춰!
16	**kick** [kik]	동 (발로) 차다 He **kicked** a stone hard. 그는 돌을 세게 찼다.
17	**knock** [nɑk]	동 두드리다, 노크하다 Someone **knocked** on the door. 누군가 문을 두드렸다.
18	**pass** [pæs]	동 지나가다 Do we have to **pass** this way? 우리는 이 길을 지나가야 하니?
19	**roll** [roul]	동 구르다, 굴리다 A potato is **rolling** down the hill. 감자 하나가 언덕을 굴러 내려가고 있다.
20	**throw** [θrou]	동 던지다 ✿ throw-threw-thrown She is **throwing** a doll high. 그녀는 인형을 높이 던지고 있다.

A 우리말 뜻과 일치하도록 빠진 글자를 써넣어 단어를 완성하세요.

1 구르다, 굴리다　　r＿＿＿＿　　　　2 점프하다　　＿u＿＿

3 던지다　　t＿＿o＿　　　　　　　　4 걸다, 매달다　　＿a＿g

5 (발로) 차다　　＿＿c＿

B 다음 영어 단어의 우리말 뜻을 쓰세요.

1 hold　＿＿＿＿＿＿＿　　　2 pass　＿＿＿＿＿＿＿

3 knock　＿＿＿＿＿＿＿　　4 hit　＿＿＿＿＿＿＿

5 hop　＿＿＿＿＿＿＿

C 우리말 뜻과 일치하도록 빈칸에 알맞은 단어를 써넣어 문장을 완성하세요.

1 Kathy ＿＿＿＿＿＿＿ the box with a stick.
　Kathy는 막대기로 그 상자를 쳤다.

2 Someone ＿＿＿＿＿＿＿ on the door.
　누군가 문을 두드렸다.

3 They were ＿＿＿＿＿＿＿ hands.
　그들은 손을 잡고 있었다.

4 A potato is ＿＿＿＿＿＿＿ down the hill.
　감자 하나가 언덕을 굴러 내려가고 있다.

5 Do we have to ＿＿＿＿＿＿＿ this way?
　우리는 이 길을 지나가야 하니?

6 I can't ＿＿＿＿＿＿＿ my shirt in the closet.
　나는 옷장에 나의 셔츠를 걸 수 없다.

7 A little girl is ＿＿＿＿＿＿＿ in the park.
　작은 소녀가 공원에서 한 발로 깡충깡충 뛰고 있다.

8 She is ＿＿＿＿＿＿＿ a doll high.
　그녀는 인형을 높이 던지고 있다.

01 brush
[brʌʃ]
명 붓
Can I borrow your brush?
너의 붓을 빌릴 수 있을까?

02 clay
[klei]
명 점토, 찰흙
I can make a car with clay.
나는 찰흙으로 자동차를 만들 수 있다.

03 color
[kʌ́lər]
명 색
Which color does she like?
그녀는 어느 색을 좋아하니?

04 colorful
[kʌ́lərfəl]
형 형형색색의, 다채로운
The flag is very colorful.
그 깃발은 색깔이 매우 다채롭다.

05 crayon
[kréiɑn]
명 크레용
Sam needs many crayons.
Sam은 많은 크레용이 필요하다.

06 design
[dizáin]
명 디자인 동 설계하다
They want a more creative design.
그들은 더 창의적인 디자인을 원한다.

07 draw
[drɔ:]
동 (연필 등으로) 그리다 ✿ draw-drew-drawn
The teacher often draws his students.
그 선생님은 자주 그의 학생들을 그린다.

08 dye
[dai]
동 염색하다
The woman dyed the cloth red.
그 여자는 그 옷감을 빨간색으로 염색했다.

09 express
[iksprés]
동 표현하다
She expresses her happiness in a painting.
그녀는 그녀의 행복을 그림으로 표현한다.

10 fold
[fould]
동 접다
He folded the letter and put it in his pocket.
그는 그 편지를 접어서 그의 주머니에 넣었다.

Daily Test

A 우리말 뜻과 일치하도록 빠진 글자를 써넣어 단어를 완성하세요.

1 색   __ o __ __ r   **2** 염색하다   d __ __

3 디자인; 설계하다   __ e __ i __ __   **4** 붓   __ __ __ s __

5 표현하다   e __ p __ __ s __

B 다음 영어 단어의 우리말 뜻을 쓰세요.

1 draw   ______________   **2** clay   ______________

3 colorful   ______________   **4** fold   ______________

5 crayon   ______________

C 우리말 뜻과 일치하도록 빈칸에 알맞은 단어를 써넣어 문장을 완성하세요.

1 I can make a car with ______________.
나는 찰흙으로 자동차를 만들 수 있다.

2 The teacher often ______________ his students.
그 선생님은 자주 그의 학생들을 그린다.

3 The flag is very ______________.
그 깃발은 색깔이 매우 다채롭다.

4 The woman ______________ the cloth red.
그 여자는 그 옷감을 빨간색으로 염색했다.

5 Sam needs many ______________.
Sam은 많은 크레용이 필요하다.

6 Which ______________ does she like?
그녀는 어느 색을 좋아하니?

7 He ______________ the letter and put it in his pocket.
그는 그 편지를 접어서 그의 주머니에 넣었다.

8 They want a more creative ______________.
그들은 더 창의적인 디자인을 원한다.

11 glue
[glu:]

명 풀, 접착제
The glue makes my hands sticky.
그 풀은 나의 손을 끈적거리게 만든다.

12 paint
[peint]

명 페인트, 그림물감   동 (그림물감으로) 그리다
What will he paint on the wall?
그는 벽에 무엇을 그릴 거니?

13 paper
[péipər]

명 종이
The butter is covered with paper.
그 버터는 종이로 싸여 있다.

14 paste
[peist]

동 붙이다
Were they pasting it on the wall?
그들은 그것을 벽에 붙이고 있었니?

15 picture
[píktʃər]

명 그림, 사진
The kid is showing her picture to Mom.
그 아이는 엄마에게 그녀의 그림을 보여 주고 있다.

16 poster
[póustər]

명 포스터, 벽보
We made the poster together.
우리는 그 포스터를 함께 만들었다.

17 scissors
[sízərz]

명 가위
I cut my finger on the scissors.
나는 그 가위에 손가락을 베었다.

18 sketchbook
[skétʃbùk]

명 스케치북
Bring your sketchbook tomorrow.
내일 너의 스케치북을 가져와.

19 statue
[stǽtʃu:]

명 조각상
This statue was made in the 1700's.
이 조각상은 1700년대에 만들어졌다.

20 tear
[tɛər]

동 찢다, 뜯다   ✿ tear-tore-torn
The dog is tearing the newspaper.
그 개는 그 신문을 찢고 있다.

Daily Test

A 우리말 뜻과 일치하도록 빠진 글자를 써넣어 단어를 완성하세요.

1 종이   __ __ p __ r   **2** 그림, 사진   __ __ __ t __ __ e

3 찢다, 뜯다   t __ a __   **4** 붙이다   __ __ s t __

5 스케치북   __ k __ __ c __ __ __ o __

B 다음 영어 단어의 우리말 뜻을 쓰세요.

1 scissors   ________________   **2** glue   ________________

3 poster   ________________   **4** statue   ________________

5 paint   ________________

C 우리말 뜻과 일치하도록 빈칸에 알맞은 단어를 써넣어 문장을 완성하세요.

1 Were they ________________ it on the wall?
그들은 그것을 벽에 붙이고 있었니?

2 We made the ________________ together.
우리는 그 포스터를 함께 만들었다.

3 The ________________ makes my hands sticky.
그 풀은 나의 손을 끈적거리게 만든다.

4 Bring your ________________ tomorrow.
내일 너의 스케치북을 가져와.

5 The kid is showing her ________________ to Mom.
그 아이는 엄마에게 그녀의 그림을 보여 주고 있다.

6 The dog is ________________ the newspaper.
그 개는 그 신문을 찢고 있다.

7 This ________________ was made in the 1700's.
이 조각상은 1700년대에 만들어졌다.

8 I cut my finger on the ________________.
나는 그 가위에 손가락을 베었다.

01 arm
[ɑ:rm]
명 팔
How many arms does the robot have?
그 로봇은 팔이 몇 개니?

02 blood
[blʌd]
명 피, 혈액 ✿ give blood 헌혈하다
I give blood once a month.
나는 한 달에 한 번 헌혈을 한다.

03 body
[bádi]
명 몸, 신체
Exercise keeps your body healthy.
운동은 너의 몸을 건강하게 유지해 준다.

04 bone
[boun]
명 뼈
We need calcium to have strong bones.
우리는 튼튼한 뼈를 갖기 위해서 칼슘이 필요하다.

05 brain
[brein]
명 뇌
Your brain is inside your head.
너의 뇌는 너의 머릿속에 있다.

06 chest
[tʃest]
명 가슴
I put a hat on my chest.
나는 모자를 나의 가슴 위에 놓았다.

07 elbow
[élbou]
명 팔꿈치
The cook hurt her elbow.
그 요리사는 팔꿈치를 다쳤다.

08 finger
[fíŋgər]
명 손가락
Was she wearing a ring on her finger?
그녀는 손가락에 반지를 끼고 있었니?

09 foot
[fut]
명 발 ✿ 복수형 feet
Wash your dirty feet with soap.
너의 더러운 발을 비누로 씻어.

10 hand
[hænd]
명 손
The hairdresser's hands moved quickly.
그 미용사의 손은 빠르게 움직였다.

A 우리말 뜻과 일치하도록 빠진 글자를 써넣어 단어를 완성하세요.

1 팔   __ r __
2 손가락   __ __ n __ __ r

3 피, 혈액   b __ __ o __
4 손   __ __ __ d

5 뼈   __ __ n __

B 다음 영어 단어의 우리말 뜻을 쓰세요.

1 chest   _______________
2 foot   _______________

3 body   _______________
4 brain   _______________

5 elbow   _______________

C 우리말 뜻과 일치하도록 빈칸에 알맞은 단어를 써넣어 문장을 완성하세요.

1 I put a hat on my _______________.
나는 모자를 나의 가슴 위에 놓았다.

2 Exercise keeps your _______________ healthy.
운동은 너의 몸을 건강하게 유지해 준다.

3 Was she wearing a ring on her _______________?
그녀는 손가락에 반지를 끼고 있었니?

4 Your _______________ is inside your head.
너의 뇌는 너의 머릿속에 있다.

5 We need calcium to have strong _______________.
우리는 튼튼한 뼈를 갖기 위해서 칼슘이 필요하다.

6 The cook hurt her _______________.
그 요리사는 팔꿈치를 다쳤다.

7 I give _______________ once a month.
나는 한 달에 한 번 헌혈을 한다.

8 How many _______________ does the robot have?
그 로봇은 팔이 몇 개니?

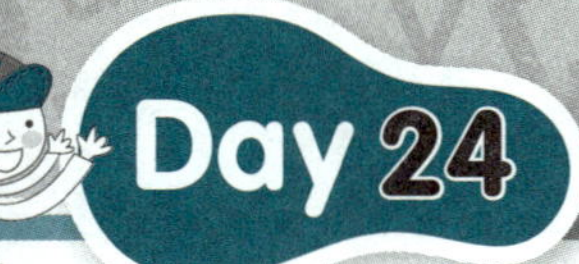

11　head
[hed]
图 머리
His head is blocking the screen.
그의 머리가 화면을 가리고 있다.

12　heart
[hɑːrt]
图 심장
What makes your heart beat fast?
무엇이 너의 심장을 빠르게 뛰게 만드니?

13　knee
[niː]
图 무릎
He hit his knee on the table.
그는 무릎을 탁자에 부딪쳤다.

14　leg
[leg]
图 다리
The woman is standing on one leg.
그 여자는 한 다리로 서 있다.

15　nail
[neil]
图 손톱
Why did you break your nail?
너는 왜 손톱을 부러뜨렸니?

16　neck
[nek]
图 목
She tied a scarf around her neck.
그녀는 목에 스카프를 맸다.

17　shoulder
[ʃóuldər]
图 어깨
Father tapped him on the shoulder.
아버지는 그의 어깨를 두드렸다.

18　toe
[tou]
图 발가락
The man didn't touch his toes.
그 남자는 발가락에 (손이) 닿지 않았다.

19　waist
[weist]
图 허리
She put on a belt around her waist.
그녀는 허리에 벨트를 맸다.

20　wrist
[rist]
图 손목, 팔목
My sister feels pain in her wrist.
나의 누나는 손목에 통증을 느낀다.

Daily Test

A 우리말 뜻과 일치하도록 빠진 글자를 써넣어 단어를 완성하세요.

1 손목, 팔목   w __ __ s __   **2** 심장   __ __ a __ t

3 손톱   __ __ __ l   **4** 발가락   t __ __

5 목   __ __ c __

B 다음 영어 단어의 우리말 뜻을 쓰세요.

1 head   _______________   **2** knee   _______________

3 shoulder   _______________   **4** waist   _______________

5 leg   _______________

C 우리말 뜻과 일치하도록 빈칸에 알맞은 단어를 써넣어 문장을 완성하세요.

1 Why did you break your _______________?
너는 왜 손톱을 부러뜨렸니?

2 He hit his _______________ on the table.
그는 무릎을 탁자에 부딪쳤다.

3 His _______________ is blocking the screen.
그의 머리가 화면을 가리고 있다.

4 She tied a scarf around her _______________.
그녀는 목에 스카프를 맸다.

5 My sister feels pain in her _______________.
나의 누나는 손목에 통증을 느낀다.

6 What makes your _______________ beat fast?
무엇이 너의 심장을 빠르게 뛰게 만드니?

7 Father tapped him on the _______________.
아버지는 그의 어깨를 두드렸다.

8 The woman is standing on one _______________.
그 여자는 한 다리로 서 있다.

A 우리말 뜻에 해당하는 영어 단어를 찾아 동그라미 하세요.

발	~해 보이다	(이로) 물다	조각상	손목, 팔목
소리가 큰	심장	접다	맛이 신	던지다

g	c	s	t	a	t	u	e	r	g
q	b	i	t	e	h	j	n	c	m
s	n	c	n	t	r	q	l	m	v
w	l	o	u	d	o	f	o	o	t
f	r	z	x	k	w	o	o	p	f
d	l	i	x	r	b	l	k	z	r
h	j	k	s	q	t	d	j	l	n
h	e	a	r	t	p	s	o	u	r

B 우리말 뜻과 일치하도록 알맞은 단어를 골라 문장을 완성하세요.

bounced	heard	crayons	spicy	bones	finger

1 He can eat ________________ food very well.
그는 매운 음식을 매우 잘 먹을 수 있다.

2 The boy ________________ the big ball.
그 소년은 그 큰 공을 튀겼다.

3 Sam needs many ________________.
Sam은 많은 크레용이 필요하다.

4 Was she wearing a ring on her ________________?
그녀는 손가락에 반지를 끼고 있었니?

5 Bill ________________ a strange voice.
Bill은 이상한 목소리를 들었다.

6 We need calcium to have strong ________________.
우리는 튼튼한 뼈를 갖기 위해서 칼슘이 필요하다.

Day 25

Day 25_C

C 들려 주는 영어 단어를 바르게 쓴 다음, 우리말 뜻을 써넣으세요.

	영어 단어	우리말		영어 단어	우리말
1			11		
2			12		
3			13		
4			14		
5			15		
6			16		
7			17		
8			18		
9			19		
10			20		

D 우리말 뜻과 일치하도록 알맞은 단어를 골라 동그라미 하세요.

1 We have five (noises / senses).
우리는 오감을 가지고 있다.

2 The man didn't touch his (toes / knees).
그 남자는 발가락에 (손이) 닿지 않았다.

3 A potato is (passing / rolling) down the hill.
감자 하나가 언덕을 굴러 내려가고 있다.

4 Bring your (sketchbook / paper) tomorrow.
내일 너의 스케치북을 가져와.

5 The hairdresser's (hands / elbows) moved quickly.
그 미용사의 손은 빠르게 움직였다.

6 They want a more creative (color / design).
그들은 더 창의적인 디자인을 원한다.

E 영어는 우리말로, 우리말은 영어로 바꿔 쓰세요.

1 colorful	_______________	2 굽히다, 구부리다	_______________
3 jump	_______________	4 풀, 접착제	_______________
5 head	_______________	6 느끼다	_______________
7 picture	_______________	8 때리다, 치다	_______________
9 salty	_______________	10 달콤한	_______________
11 clap	_______________	12 염색하다	_______________
13 float	_______________	14 허리	_______________
15 neck	_______________	16 피, 혈액	_______________
17 knock	_______________	18 종이	_______________
19 smell	_______________	20 뇌	_______________

Day 25_F

F 잘 듣고, 빈칸에 알맞은 단어를 써넣어 문장을 완성하세요.

1 The birds are _______________ between the houses.

2 We made the _______________ together.

3 This cream has an orange _______________ .

4 What's that _______________ in the hall?

5 Why did you break your _______________ ?

6 This pumpkin pie _______________ good.

7 Do we have to _______________ this way?

8 Which _______________ does she like?

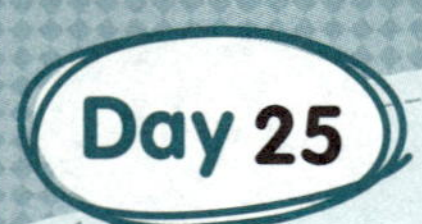

Day 25

G 우리말 뜻과 일치하도록 빈칸에 알맞은 단어를 써넣어 문장을 완성하세요.

1 How many a________________ does the robot have?
그 로봇은 팔이 몇 개니?

2 The steak was really d________________.
그 스테이크는 정말 맛있었다.

3 Can I borrow your b________________?
너의 붓을 빌릴 수 있을까?

4 We should c________________ our food well.
우리는 음식을 잘 씹어야 한다.

5 The dog was s________________ at the box.
그 개는 그 상자의 냄새를 맡고 있었다.

6 The cook hurt her e________________.
그 요리사는 팔꿈치를 다쳤다.

7 My friends d________________ into the water.
나의 친구들은 물속으로 다이빙했다.

8 The woman is standing on one l________________.
그 여자는 한 다리로 서 있다.

9 A little girl is h________________ in the park.
작은 소녀가 공원에서 한 발로 깡충깡충 뛰고 있다.

10 I cut my finger on the s________________.
나는 그 가위에 손가락을 베었다.

Review에서 틀린 문제의 영어 단어와 우리말 뜻을 쓴 다음, 영어 단어를 3번씩 쓰세요.

01 arrow
[ǽrou]

명 화살표
Follow those arrows, and you can find treasures.
저 화살표를 따라가, 그러면 너는 보물을 찾을 수 있어.

02 black
[blæk]

명 검은색   형 검은
His black hat looks great.
그의 검은색 모자는 정말 멋져 보인다.

03 blue
[bluː]

명 파란색   형 파란
They painted the fence blue.
그들은 그 울타리를 파란색으로 칠했다.

04 brown
[braun]

명 갈색   형 갈색의
The brown pencil is under the chair.
그 갈색 연필은 의자 아래에 있다.

05 circle
[sə́ːrkl]

명 원형, 동그라미
Make a circle with your hands.
너의 손으로 동그라미를 만들어.

06 cube
[kjuːb]

명 정육면체
This large box is a cube.
이 큰 상자는 정육면체이다.

07 gray
[grei]

명 회색   형 회색의
The teenager bought those gray sneakers.
그 십 대는 저 회색 운동화를 샀다.

08 green
[griːn]

명 녹색   형 녹색의
We enjoy watching the green leaves.
우리는 그 녹색 잎들을 보는 것을 즐긴다.

09 pink
[piŋk]

명 분홍색   형 분홍색의
I saw a pink dolphin on TV.
나는 TV에서 분홍색 돌고래를 봤다.

10 purple
[pə́ːrpl]

명 자주색   형 자주색의
The purple flower is my favorite.
그 자주색 꽃이 내가 가장 좋아하는 것이다.

Daily Test

A 우리말 뜻과 일치하도록 빠진 글자를 써넣어 단어를 완성하세요.

1 정육면체   c __ b __   **2** 화살표   a __ __ __ w

3 검은색; 검은   __ l __ __ __ __   **4** 자주색; 자주색의   __ u r __ __ __

5 녹색; 녹색의   __ __ e __ n

B 다음 영어 단어의 우리말 뜻을 쓰세요.

1 brown   _______________   **2** pink   _______________

3 blue   _______________   **4** gray   _______________

5 circle   _______________

C 우리말 뜻과 일치하도록 빈칸에 알맞은 단어를 써넣어 문장을 완성하세요.

1 They painted the fence _______________.
그들은 그 울타리를 파란색으로 칠했다.

2 His _______________ hat looks great.
그의 검은 모자는 정말 멋져 보인다.

3 This large box is a _______________.
이 큰 상자는 정육면체이다.

4 I saw a _______________ dolphin on TV.
나는 TV에서 분홍색 돌고래를 봤다.

5 The _______________ pencil is under the chair.
그 갈색 연필은 의자 아래에 있다.

6 Follow those _______________, and you can find treasures.
저 화살표를 따라가, 그러면 너는 보물을 찾을 수 있어.

7 The _______________ flower is my favorite.
그 자주색 꽃이 내가 가장 좋아하는 것이다.

8 We enjoy watching the _______________ leaves.
우리는 그 녹색 잎들을 보는 것을 즐긴다.

11 rectangle
[réktæ̀ŋgl]

명 직사각형
The child folded the towel into a rectangle.
그 어린이는 그 수건을 직사각형으로 접었다.

12 red
[red]

명 빨간색 형 빨간색의
Chinese people like red, don't they?
중국 사람들은 빨간색을 좋아해, 그렇지 않니?

13 round
[raund]

형 둥근, 원형의
The family will have dinner at the round table.
그 가족은 그 둥근 탁자에서 저녁을 먹을 것이다.

14 shape
[ʃeip]

명 모양
Cut the paper in a heart shape.
그 종이를 하트 모양으로 잘라.

15 square
[skwɛər]

명 정사각형
Let's draw a square on the ground.
땅바닥에 정사각형 하나를 그리자.

16 star
[staːr]

명 별 모양
I put a star sticker on my notebook.
나는 나의 공책에 별 모양 스티커를 붙였다.

17 straight
[streit]

부 똑바로 형 곧은, 똑바른
They are walking along the straight line.
그들은 그 곧은 선을 따라 걷고 있다.

18 triangle
[tráiæ̀ŋgl]

명 삼각형
I'm looking for a small triangle.
나는 작은 삼각형을 찾고 있다.

19 white
[hwait]

명 흰색 형 흰색의
The bread is as white as snow.
그 빵은 눈처럼 하얗다.

20 yellow
[jélou]

명 노란색 형 노란색의
Did the driver see the yellow light?
그 운전사는 그 노란색 불을 봤니?

A 우리말 뜻과 일치하도록 빠진 글자를 써넣어 단어를 완성하세요.

1 흰색; 흰색의   __ h __ __ e   2 모양   __ h __ p __

3 별 모양   s __ __ __   4 둥근, 원형의   r __ u __ __

5 빨간색; 빨간색의   __ __ d

B 다음 영어 단어의 우리말 뜻을 쓰세요.

1 square   2 yellow

3 straight   4 triangle

5 rectangle

C 우리말 뜻과 일치하도록 빈칸에 알맞은 단어를 써넣어 문장을 완성하세요.

1 Let's draw a ________________ on the ground.
땅바닥에 정사각형 하나를 그리자.

2 The family will have dinner at the ________________ table.
그 가족은 그 둥근 탁자에서 저녁을 먹을 것이다.

3 They are walking along the ________________ line.
그들은 그 곧은 선을 따라 걷고 있다.

4 The child folded the towel into a ________________.
그 어린이는 그 수건을 직사각형으로 접었다.

5 Cut the paper in a heart ________________.
그 종이를 하트 모양으로 잘라.

6 Did the driver see the ________________ light?
그 운전사는 그 노란색 불을 봤니?

7 I'm looking for a small ________________.
나는 작은 삼각형을 찾고 있다.

8 Chinese people like ________________, don't they?
중국 사람들은 빨간색을 좋아해, 그렇지 않니?

01 eleven
[ilévən]

명 11, 열하나
The cat is eleven years old.
그 고양이는 11살이다.

02 twelve
[twelv]

명 12, 열둘
I was making twelve sandwiches then.
나는 그때 샌드위치 12개를 만들고 있었다.

03 thirteen
[θə̀ːrtíːn]

명 13, 열셋
Thirteen years later, the girl became an actress.
13년 후에, 그 소녀는 여배우가 되었다.

04 fourteen
[fɔ̀ːrtíːn]

명 14, 열넷
The fourteen seats are not taken.
좌석이 14개 비어 있다.

05 fifteen
[fìftíːn]

명 15, 열다섯
Does Jack take care of fifteen sheep?
Jack은 양 15마리를 돌보니?

06 sixteen
[sìkstíːn]

명 16, 열여섯
Where did you travel for sixteen days?
너는 16일 동안 어디를 여행했니?

07 seventeen
[sèvəntíːn]

명 17, 열일곱
He feeds seventeen dogs every day.
그는 매일 개 17마리에게 먹이를 준다.

08 eighteen
[èitíːn]

명 18, 열여덟
Ann collected eighteen necklaces.
Ann은 목걸이 18개를 모았다.

09 nineteen
[nàintíːn]

명 19, 열아홉
The park has nineteen benches.
그 공원에는 벤치가 19개 있다.

10 twenty
[twénti]

명 20, 스물
How did she find the twenty notebooks?
그녀는 어떻게 그 공책 20권을 찾았니?

A 우리말 뜻과 일치하도록 빠진 글자를 써넣어 단어를 완성하세요.

1 13, 열셋   _ _ i _ t _ _ _ _

2 20, 스물   t _ _ n _ _ _

3 16, 열여섯   s _ _ t _ _ _ _

4 12, 열둘   _ _ e _ v _

5 19, 열아홉   _ _ _ e t _ _ _ _

B 다음 영어 단어의 우리말 뜻을 쓰세요.

1 eleven   _________________

2 fifteen   _________________

3 eighteen   _________________

4 fourteen   _________________

5 seventeen   _________________

C 우리말 뜻과 일치하도록 빈칸에 알맞은 단어를 써넣어 문장을 완성하세요.

1 How did she find the _________________ notebooks?
그녀는 어떻게 그 공책 20권을 찾았니?

2 I was making _________________ sandwiches then.
나는 그때 샌드위치 12개를 만들고 있었다.

3 Where did you travel for _________________ days?
너는 16일 동안 어디를 여행했니?

4 Ann collected _________________ necklaces.
Ann은 목걸이 18개를 모았다.

5 The cat is _________________ years old.
그 고양이는 11살이다.

6 He feeds _________________ dogs every day.
그는 매일 개 17마리에게 먹이를 준다.

7 Does Jack take care of _________________ sheep?
Jack은 양 15마리를 돌보니?

8 _________________ years later, the girl became an actress.
13년 후에, 그 소녀는 여배우가 되었다.

11	**thirty** [θə́ːrti]	명 30, 서른 Thirty children sit around the teacher. 어린이 30명이 그 선생님 주위에 앉는다.
12	**forty** [fɔ́ːrti]	명 40, 마흔 Will they taste the forty glasses of juice? 그들은 그 주스 40잔을 맛볼 거니?
13	**fifty** [fífti]	명 50, 쉰 We have to jump rope fifty times. 우리는 줄넘기를 50번 해야 한다.
14	**sixty** [síksti]	명 60, 예순 The glasses cost sixty dollars. 그 안경은 60달러이다.
15	**seventy** [sévənti]	명 70, 일흔 Open your book to page seventy. 너의 책 70쪽을 펴.
16	**eighty** [éiti]	명 80, 여든 The eighty students are walking toward the stage. 그 80명의 학생들이 무대 쪽으로 걸어가고 있다.
17	**ninety** [náinti]	명 90, 아흔 The kids planted ninety trees. 그 아이들은 나무 90그루를 심었다.
18	**hundred** [hʌ́ndrəd]	명 100, 백 Grandma created one hundred paintings. 할머니는 100점의 그림을 그리셨다.
19	**thousand** [θáuzənd]	명 1,000, 천 Two thousand people can stay at this hotel. 2,000명의 사람들이 이 호텔에서 묵을 수 있다.
20	**number** [nʌ́mbər]	명 수, 숫자 Seven is my lucky number. 7은 나의 행운의 숫자이다.

Daily Test

A 우리말 뜻과 일치하도록 빠진 글자를 써넣어 단어를 완성하세요.

1 70, 일흔   s _ _ _ n _ y

2 수, 숫자   _ u m _ _ _

3 40, 마흔   _ _ r _ y

4 100, 백   h _ n _ _ e _

5 50, 쉰   f _ f _ _

B 다음 영어 단어의 우리말 뜻을 쓰세요.

1 sixty _________________

2 thirty _________________

3 thousand _________________

4 eighty _________________

5 ninety _________________

C 우리말 뜻과 일치하도록 빈칸에 알맞은 단어를 써넣어 문장을 완성하세요.

1 Open your book to page _________________.
너의 책 70쪽을 펴.

2 _________________ children sit around the teacher.
어린이 30명이 그 선생님 주위에 앉는다.

3 Two _________________ people can stay at this hotel.
2,000명의 사람들이 이 호텔에서 묵을 수 있다.

4 Will they taste the _________________ glasses of juice?
그들은 그 주스 40잔을 맛볼 거니?

5 The kids planted _________________ trees.
그 아이들은 나무 90그루를 심었다.

6 We have to jump rope _________________ times.
우리는 줄넘기를 50번 해야 한다.

7 Seven is my lucky _________________.
7은 나의 행운의 숫자이다.

8 The _________________ students are walking toward the stage.
그 80명의 학생들이 무대 쪽으로 걸어가고 있다.

01 basket
[bǽskit]
명 바구니
The basket is full of fruits.
그 바구니는 과일들로 가득 차 있다.

02 blanket
[blǽŋkit]
명 담요
I'll give him some blankets.
나는 그에게 담요 몇 장을 줄 것이다.

03 bottle
[bátl]
명 병
Did she pour juice into the bottles?
그녀는 그 병들에 주스를 부었니?

04 bowl
[boul]
명 그릇
Which bowl do they want, green or red?
그들은 녹색과 빨간색 중 어느 그릇을 원하니?

05 chopsticks
[tʃápstiks]
명 젓가락
How about using these chopsticks?
이 젓가락들을 사용하는 게 어때?

06 cup
[kʌp]
명 컵, 잔
The girl is looking for her favorite cup.
그 소녀는 그녀가 가장 좋아하는 컵을 찾고 있다.

07 dish
[diʃ]
명 접시
Please take out the big dish.
그 큰 접시를 꺼내 주세요.

08 fork
[fɔːrk]
명 포크
The kid should eat with a fork.
그 아이는 포크로 먹는 게 좋겠다.

09 glass
[glæs]
명 유리잔
He dropped the glass on the floor.
그는 그 유리잔을 바닥에 떨어뜨렸다.

10 hammer
[hǽmər]
명 망치
The store sells hammers.
그 가게는 망치를 판다.

Daily Test

A 우리말 뜻과 일치하도록 빠진 글자를 써넣어 단어를 완성하세요.

1 접시   __ __ __ h

2 유리잔   g __ __ s __

3 포크   __ __ __ k

4 바구니   __ a __ __ __ t

5 그릇   b __ w __

B 다음 영어 단어의 우리말 뜻을 쓰세요.

1 hammer   _________________

2 blanket   _________________

3 chopsticks   _________________

4 bottle   _________________

5 cup   _________________

C 우리말 뜻과 일치하도록 빈칸에 알맞은 단어를 써넣어 문장을 완성하세요.

1 Which _________________ do they want, green or red?
그들은 녹색과 빨간색 중 어느 그릇을 원하니?

2 The kid should eat with a _________________.
그 아이는 포크로 먹는 게 좋겠다.

3 The _________________ is full of fruits.
그 바구니는 과일들로 가득 차 있다.

4 The girl is looking for her favorite _________________.
그 소녀는 그녀가 가장 좋아하는 컵을 찾고 있다.

5 I'll give him some _________________.
나는 그에게 담요 몇 장을 줄 것이다.

6 He dropped the _________________ on the floor.
그는 그 유리잔을 바닥에 떨어뜨렸다.

7 How about using these _________________?
이 젓가락들을 사용하는 게 어때?

8 The store sells _________________.
그 가게는 망치를 판다.

11 jar
[dʒɑːr]

명 병, 단지
I put strawberry jam in the jar.
나는 그 병에 딸기 잼을 넣었다.

12 key
[kiː]

명 열쇠
I don't remember where the key is.
나는 그 열쇠가 어디에 있는지 기억나지 않는다.

13 knife
[naif]

명 칼
Please be careful with the knife.
그 칼은 조심하세요.

14 ladder
[lǽdər]

명 사다리
Grandpa is climbing up the ladder.
할아버지는 그 사다리를 올라가고 계신다.

15 lamp
[læmp]

명 램프
We turned on the lamp in the dark.
우리는 어둠 속에서 램프를 켰다.

16 shelf
[ʃelf]

명 선반
I put the book on the shelf.
나는 그 책을 선반에 놓았다.

17 soap
[soup]

명 비누
This soap smells very good.
이 비누는 매우 좋은 냄새가 난다.

18 spoon
[spuːn]

명 숟가락
This spoon is too big for the baby.
이 숟가락은 그 아기에게는 너무 크다.

19 towel
[táuəl]

명 수건
Hang the towel on the hook.
그 수건을 고리에 걸어.

20 umbrella
[ʌmbrélə]

명 우산
Is that umbrella yours?
저 우산은 너의 것이니?

Daily Test

A 우리말 뜻과 일치하도록 빠진 글자를 써넣어 단어를 완성하세요.

1 병, 단지   j __ __   2 사다리   __ __ d __ e __

3 수건   t __ w __ __   4 비누   __ o __ __

5 칼   __ __ __ f __

B 다음 영어 단어의 우리말 뜻을 쓰세요.

1 umbrella   _________________   2 key   _________________

3 spoon   _________________   4 lamp   _________________

5 shelf   _________________

C 우리말 뜻과 일치하도록 빈칸에 알맞은 단어를 써넣어 문장을 완성하세요.

1 Grandpa is climbing up the _________________.
할아버지는 그 사다리를 올라가고 계신다.

2 Is that _________________ yours?
저 우산은 너의 것이니?

3 This _________________ smells very good.
이 비누는 매우 좋은 냄새가 난다.

4 I don't remember where the _________________ is.
나는 그 열쇠가 어디에 있는지 기억나지 않는다.

5 Hang the _________________ on the hook.
그 수건을 고리에 걸어.

6 Please be careful with the _________________.
그 칼은 조심하세요.

7 This _________________ is too big for the baby.
이 숟가락은 그 아기에게는 너무 크다.

8 We turned on the _________________ in the dark.
우리는 어둠 속에서 램프를 켰다.

01 actor
[ǽktər]
명 배우
The actor appeared in the movie.
그 배우는 그 영화에 출연했다.

02 actress
[ǽktris]
명 여배우
The actress wrote a script about her life.
그 여배우는 그녀의 인생에 대한 대본을 썼다.

03 artist
[ά:rtist]
명 화가, 예술가
Monet is a beloved artist all over the world.
모네는 세계적으로 사랑받는 화가이다.

04 baker
[béikər]
명 제빵사
The baker's bread was sold out in an hour.
그 제빵사의 빵은 한 시간 내에 다 팔렸다.

05 cook
[kuk]
명 요리사
What kind of food is the cook good at?
그 요리사는 어떤 종류의 음식을 잘하니?

06 dancer
[dǽnsər]
명 무용수
I want to be a ballet dancer.
나는 발레 무용수가 되고 싶다.

07 designer
[dizáinər]
명 디자이너
James was an excellent designer.
James는 훌륭한 디자이너였다.

08 doctor
[dάktər]
명 의사
Would you call a doctor?
의사를 불러 주시겠습니까?

09 farmer
[fά:rmər]
명 농부
Some farmers grow rice there.
어떤 농부들은 거기에서 벼를 기른다.

10 job
[dʒab]
명 일, 직업
New jobs will be created in the future.
미래에는 새로운 직업들이 생겨날 것이다.

Daily Test

A 우리말 뜻과 일치하도록 빠진 글자를 써넣어 단어를 완성하세요.

1 제빵사   b __ __ e __

2 의사   __ __ c __ __ r

3 화가, 예술가   __ r __ i __ __

4 일, 직업   j __ __

5 배우   __ __ t __ r

B 다음 영어 단어의 우리말 뜻을 쓰세요.

1 actress   __________________

2 dancer   __________________

3 cook   __________________

4 farmer   __________________

5 designer   __________________

C 우리말 뜻과 일치하도록 빈칸에 알맞은 단어를 써넣어 문장을 완성하세요.

1 The __________________ appeared in the movie.
그 배우는 그 영화에 출연했다.

2 Monet is a beloved __________________ all over the world.
모네는 세계적으로 사랑받는 화가이다.

3 I want to be a ballet __________________.
나는 발레 무용수가 되고 싶다.

4 Some __________________ grow rice there.
어떤 농부들은 거기에서 벼를 기른다.

5 New __________________ will be created in the future.
미래에는 새로운 직업들이 생겨날 것이다.

6 James was an excellent __________________.
James는 훌륭한 디자이너였다.

7 What kind of food is the __________________ good at?
그 요리사는 어떤 종류의 음식을 잘하니?

8 The __________________ wrote a script about her life.
그 여배우는 그녀의 인생에 대한 대본을 썼다.

11 magician
[mədʒíʃən]

명 마술사
The magician is behind the curtain.
그 마술사는 커튼 뒤에 있다.

12 model
[mádəl]

명 모델
Models in funny clothes showed up.
우스꽝스러운 옷을 입은 모델들이 나타났다.

13 musician
[mju(:)zíʃən]

명 음악가
A musician is singing on the street.
한 음악가가 거리에서 노래를 부르고 있다.

14 nurse
[nə:rs]

명 간호사
There aren't any nurses in the hospital.
그 병원에는 간호사가 한 명도 없다.

15 pilot
[páilət]

명 비행기 조종사
The pilot is checking the plane.
그 비행기 조종사는 그 비행기를 점검하고 있다.

16 scientist
[sáiəntist]

명 과학자
The scientist finished the experiment.
그 과학자는 그 실험을 마쳤다.

17 singer
[síŋər]

명 가수
The singer has a concert once a year.
그 가수는 일 년에 한 번씩 콘서트를 한다.

18 teacher
[tí:tʃər]

명 선생님
Kathy likes the teacher's art class.
Kathy는 그 선생님의 미술 수업을 좋아한다.

19 vet
[vet]

명 수의사
Take your bird to the vet.
너의 새를 수의사에게 데려가.

20 writer
[ráitər]

명 작가
Jake recommended the writer's book.
Jake는 그 작가의 책을 추천했다.

Daily Test

A 우리말 뜻과 일치하도록 빠진 글자를 써넣어 단어를 완성하세요.

1 선생님   _ _ _ c _ e _　　**2** 간호사   _ u _ _ e

3 모델   _ o _ e _　　**4** 작가   w _ _ t _ _

5 가수   _ i _ _ _ r

B 다음 영어 단어의 우리말 뜻을 쓰세요.

1 magician   _________________　　**2** scientist   _________________

3 vet   _________________　　**4** pilot   _________________

5 musician   _________________

C 우리말 뜻과 일치하도록 빈칸에 알맞은 단어를 써넣어 문장을 완성하세요.

1 _________________ in funny clothes showed up.
우스꽝스러운 옷을 입은 모델들이 나타났다.

2 The _________________ is behind the curtain.
그 마술사는 커튼 뒤에 있다.

3 The _________________ finished the experiment.
그 과학자는 그 실험을 마쳤다.

4 Take your bird to the _________________.
너의 새를 수의사에게 데려가.

5 There aren't any _________________ in the hospital.
그 병원에는 간호사가 한 명도 없다.

6 The _________________ is checking the plane.
그 비행기 조종사는 그 비행기를 점검하고 있다.

7 A _________________ is singing on the street.
한 음악가가 거리에서 노래를 부르고 있다.

8 The _________________ has a concert once a year.
그 가수는 일 년에 한 번씩 콘서트를 한다.

Day 30 Review | Day 26~29

A 우리말 뜻에 해당하는 영어 단어를 찾아 동그라미 하세요.

12, 열둘	녹색; 녹색의	배우	포크	칼
모양	램프	정육면체	50, 쉰	간호사

t	s	g	z	x	k	f	o	r	k
w	y	q	r	k	c	u	b	e	b
e	h	g	g	e	r	s	f	f	y
l	k	n	i	f	e	z	u	i	a
v	f	u	q	d	u	n	l	f	c
e	q	r	r	j	l	q	a	t	t
w	k	s	h	a	p	e	m	y	o
h	z	e	u	g	t	t	p	l	r

B 우리말 뜻과 일치하도록 알맞은 단어를 골라 문장을 완성하세요.

straight	sixteen	bottles	brown	designer	ninety

1 The _________________ pencil is under the chair.
그 갈색 연필은 의자 아래에 있다.

2 They are walking along the _________________ line.
그들은 그 곧은 선을 따라 걷고 있다.

3 James was an excellent _________________.
James는 훌륭한 디자이너였다.

4 Where did you travel for _________________ days?
너는 16일 동안 어디를 여행했니?

5 Did she pour juice into the _________________?
그녀는 그 병들에 주스를 부었니?

6 The kids planted _________________ trees.
그 아이들은 나무 90그루를 심었다.

Day 30

Day 30_C

C 들려 주는 영어 단어를 바르게 쓴 다음, 우리말 뜻을 써넣으세요.

	영어 단어	우리말		영어 단어	우리말
1			11		
2			12		
3			13		
4			14		
5			15		
6			16		
7			17		
8			18		
9			19		
10			20		

D 우리말 뜻과 일치하도록 알맞은 단어를 골라 동그라미 하세요.

1. I want to be a ballet (writer / dancer).
   나는 발레 무용수가 되고 싶다.

2. The bread is as (yellow / white) as snow.
   그 빵은 눈처럼 하얗다.

3. Open your book to page (seventy / seventeen).
   너의 책 70쪽을 펴.

4. Grandpa is climbing up the (ladder / shelf).
   할아버지는 그 사다리를 올라가고 계신다.

5. Kathy likes the (scientist's / teacher's) art class.
   Kathy는 그 선생님의 미술 수업을 좋아한다.

6. Please take out the big (dish / glass).
   그 큰 접시를 꺼내 주세요.

E 영어는 우리말로, 우리말은 영어로 바꿔 쓰세요.

1	jar	__________	**2** 삼각형	__________
3	thirteen	__________	**4** 컵, 잔	__________
5	circle	__________	**6** 우산	__________
7	baker	__________	**8** 수, 숫자	__________
9	eighty	__________	**10** 가수	__________
11	shelf	__________	**12** 17, 열일곱	__________
13	magician	__________	**14** 회색; 회색의	__________
15	nineteen	__________	**16** 숟가락	__________
17	square	__________	**18** 의사	__________
19	writer	__________	**20** 30, 서른	__________

Day 30_F

F 잘 듣고, 빈칸에 알맞은 단어를 써넣어 문장을 완성하세요.

1 The cat is __________ years old.

2 Follow those __________, and you can find treasures.

3 I saw a __________ dolphin on TV.

4 The __________ wrote a script about her life.

5 The store sells __________.

6 The __________ is full of fruits.

7 A __________ is singing on the street.

8 Chinese people like __________, don't they?

Day 30

G 우리말 뜻과 일치하도록 빈칸에 알맞은 단어를 써넣어 문장을 완성하세요.

1 The p_________________ is checking the plane.
그 비행기 조종사는 그 비행기를 점검하고 있다.

2 His b_______________ hat looks great.
그의 검은 모자는 정말 멋져 보인다.

3 The child folded the towel into a r_______________.
그 어린이는 그 수건을 직사각형으로 접었다.

4 Does Jack take care of f_______________ sheep?
Jack은 양 15마리를 돌보니?

5 The s_______________ finished the experiment.
그 과학자는 그 실험을 마쳤다.

6 Grandma created one h_______________ paintings.
할머니는 100점의 그림을 그리셨다.

7 I'll give him some b_______________.
나는 그에게 담요 몇 장을 줄 것이다.

8 This s_______________ smells very good.
이 비누는 매우 좋은 냄새가 난다.

9 Some f_______________ grow rice there.
어떤 농부들은 거기에서 벼를 기른다.

10 Will they taste the f_______________ glasses of juice?
그들은 그 주스 40잔을 맛볼 거니?

✎ Review에서 틀린 문제의 영어 단어와 우리말 뜻을 쓴 다음, 영어 단어를 3번씩 쓰세요.

	(	)	______	______ ______
	(	)	______	______ ______
	(	)	______	______ ______
	(	)	______	______ ______
	(	)	______	______ ______

Phonics Check

Day 31~35

모르는 단어라서 읽을 수 없다고요?
Phonics를 알면 어떤 단어도 읽을 수 있어요.
Phonics 점검을 통해 영어 자신감을 길러요.

Check! Word family별로 단어를 읽어 보세요.

01 fail
[feil]
동 실패하다 ✿ fail in ~에 실패하다
I failed in the exam.
나는 그 시험에 실패했다.

02 jail
[ʤeil]
명 교도소, 감옥
He finally got out of the jail.
그는 드디어 감옥에서 나왔다.

03 mail
[meil]
명 우편, 우편물
Let's send this book by mail.
이 책을 우편으로 보내자.

04 nail
[neil]
명 손톱
I bite my nails when I'm nervous.
나는 긴장했을 때 나의 손톱을 물어뜯는다.

05 rail
[reil]
명 난간, 철도 레일
You must not lean on the rail.
너희는 난간에 기대면 안 된다.

06 retail
[ríːteil]
명 소매
They work at a retail store.
그들은 소매점에서 일한다.

07 sail
[seil]
동 항해하다 명 돛
Columbus sailed to find India.
콜럼버스는 인도를 찾기 위해 항해했다.

08 snail
[sneil]
명 달팽이
A snail has a hard shell on its back.
달팽이는 등에 단단한 껍데기가 있다.

09 tail
[teil]
명 꼬리
Paul's dog wagged its tail.
Paul의 개가 꼬리를 흔들었다.

10 trail
[treil]
명 오솔길, 산길
She jogs on this trail in the morning.
그녀는 아침에 이 오솔길에서 조깅을 한다.

Daily Test

A 우리말 뜻과 일치하도록 빠진 글자를 써넣어 단어를 완성하세요.

1 교도소, 감옥   __ a __ l

2 오솔길, 산길   t __ a __ __

3 실패하다   __ __ i __

4 달팽이   __ n __ __ l

5 항해하다; 돛   s __ __ __

B 다음 영어 단어의 우리말 뜻을 쓰세요.

1 nail _________________

2 retail _________________

3 mail _________________

4 tail _________________

5 rail _________________

C 우리말 뜻과 일치하도록 빈칸에 알맞은 단어를 써넣어 문장을 완성하세요.

1 He finally got out of the _________________.
그는 드디어 감옥에서 나왔다.

2 They work at a _________________ store.
그들은 소매점에서 일한다.

3 Let's send this book by _________________.
이 책을 우편으로 보내자.

4 She jogs on this _________________ in the morning.
그녀는 아침에 이 오솔길에서 조깅을 한다.

5 Columbus _________________ to find India.
콜럼버스는 인도를 찾기 위해 항해했다.

6 I _________________ in the exam.
나는 그 시험에 실패했다.

7 A _________________ has a hard shell on its back.
달팽이는 등에 단단한 껍데기가 있다.

8 You must not lean on the _________________.
너희는 난간에 기대면 안 된다.

11 again
[əgéin]

부 다시
I read the book again.
나는 그 책을 다시 읽었다.

12 brain
[brein]

명 뇌
A brain controls your body.
뇌는 너의 몸을 조절한다.

13 contain
[kəntéin]

동 ~이 들어 있다
A tomato contains much water.
토마토에는 많은 수분이 들어 있다.

14 gain
[gein]

동 얻다
She started to gain weight.
그녀는 살이 찌기 시작했다.

15 grain
[grein]

명 곡물, 낟알
Do you know the name of the grain?
너는 그 곡물의 이름을 아니?

16 main
[mein]

형 주된
Steak will be the main course today.
스테이크가 오늘 주요리가 될 것이다.

17 pain
[pein]

명 아픔, 통증
Massage can reduce your pain.
마사지는 너의 통증을 줄여 줄 수 있다.

18 rain
[rein]

명 비 동 비가 오다
The laundry doesn't dry well when it rains.
비가 올 때는 빨래가 잘 마르지 않는다.

19 remain
[riméin]

동 계속 ~이다
The men remained silent.
그 남자들은 계속 조용히 있었다.

20 train
[trein]

명 기차, 열차
Which train leaves earlier?
어느 기차가 더 일찍 출발하니?

131

Daily Test

A 우리말 뜻과 일치하도록 빠진 글자를 써넣어 단어를 완성하세요.

1 곡물, 낟알   __ r __ __ n

2 기차, 열차   t __ a __ __

3 다시   __ __ a __ __

4 비; 비가 오다   __ __ __ n

5 ~이 들어 있다   c __ __ __ __ i __

B 다음 영어 단어의 우리말 뜻을 쓰세요.

1 brain   ________________

2 pain   ________________

3 remain   ________________

4 gain   ________________

5 main   ________________

C 우리말 뜻과 일치하도록 빈칸에 알맞은 단어를 써넣어 문장을 완성하세요.

1 A ________________ controls your body.
뇌는 너의 몸을 조절한다.

2 The laundry doesn't dry well when it ________________.
비가 올 때는 빨래가 잘 마르지 않는다.

3 Steak will be the ________________ course today.
스테이크가 오늘 주요리가 될 것이다.

4 I read the book ________________.
나는 그 책을 다시 읽었다.

5 Which ________________ leaves earlier?
어느 기차가 더 일찍 출발하니?

6 Do you know the name of the ________________?
너는 그 곡물의 이름을 아니?

7 Massage can reduce your ________________.
마사지는 너의 통증을 줄여 줄 수 있다.

8 A tomato ________________ much water.
토마토에는 많은 수분이 들어 있다.

01 beat
[biːt]

동 이기다 ✿ beat-beat-beaten
Korea beat China by two points.
한국이 중국을 2점 차로 이겼다.

02 cheat
[tʃiːt]

동 속이다, 부정행위를 하다
Cheating in the exam isn't fair.
시험에서 부정행위를 하는 것은 공정하지 않다.

03 eat
[iːt]

동 먹다 ✿ eat-ate-eaten
What did you eat for lunch?
너는 점심으로 무엇을 먹었니?

04 heat
[hiːt]

명 열
The heat melted the snow.
그 열이 눈을 녹였다.

05 meat
[miːt]

명 고기
The woman is cutting meat with a knife.
그 여자는 칼로 고기를 자르고 있다.

06 neat
[niːt]

형 단정한
You look neat after brushing your hair.
너는 머리를 빗으니 단정해 보인다.

07 repeat
[ripíːt]

동 반복하다, 한 번 더 말하다
Could you repeat that?
다시 말씀해 주시겠어요?

08 seat
[siːt]

명 자리, 좌석
Please have a seat.
자리에 앉으세요.

09 treat
[triːt]

동 대하다, 취급하다
Our parents treat us all the same.
우리 부모님은 우리를 똑같이 대하신다.

10 wheat
[hwiːt]

명 밀
Flour is made from wheat.
밀가루는 밀로 만든다.

Daily Test

A 우리말 뜻과 일치하도록 빠진 글자를 써넣어 단어를 완성하세요.

1 밀   w __ __ a __   2 단정한   __ __ __ t

3 자리, 좌석   s __ __ __   4 이기다   __ __ a __

5 먹다   __ __ t

B 다음 영어 단어의 우리말 뜻을 쓰세요.

1 repeat   __________________   2 treat   __________________

3 cheat   __________________   4 meat   __________________

5 heat   __________________

C 우리말 뜻과 일치하도록 빈칸에 알맞은 단어를 써넣어 문장을 완성하세요.

1 The woman is cutting _________________ with a knife.
그 여자는 칼로 고기를 자르고 있다.

2 Korea _________________ China by two points.
한국이 중국을 2점 차로 이겼다.

3 What did you _________________ for lunch?
너는 점심으로 무엇을 먹었니?

4 You look _________________ after brushing your hair.
너는 머리를 빗으니 단정해 보인다.

5 Flour is made from _________________.
밀가루는 밀로 만든다.

6 _________________ in the exam isn't fair.
시험에서 부정행위를 하는 것은 공정하지 않다.

7 Our parents _________________ us all the same.
우리 부모님은 우리를 똑같이 대하신다.

8 The _________________ melted the snow.
그 열이 눈을 녹였다.

11 bleed [bliːd]
동 피가 나다, 피를 흘리다 ✿ bleed-bled-bled
Her forehead is bleeding.
그녀의 이마에서 피가 나고 있다.

12 exceed [iksíːd]
동 넘다, 초과하다
The price will not exceed 50 dollars.
그 가격은 50달러를 넘지 않을 것이다.

13 feed [fiːd]
동 먹이를 주다 ✿ feed-fed-fed
What time should I feed the horses?
내가 몇 시에 그 말들에게 먹이를 줘야 하니?

14 greed [griːd]
명 탐욕
We have to control our greed.
우리는 욕심을 제어해야 한다.

15 indeed [indíːd]
부 정말, 참으로
The musical was fantastic indeed.
그 뮤지컬은 정말 환상적이었다.

16 need [niːd]
동 필요로 하다
Which tool does the carpenter need?
그 목수는 어느 도구가 필요하니?

17 seed [siːd]
명 씨, 씨앗
These seeds will grow into sunflowers.
이 씨앗들은 자라서 해바라기가 될 것이다.

18 speed [spiːd]
명 속도
She is driving the bus at low speed.
그녀는 낮은 속도로 버스를 운전하고 있다.

19 succeed [səksíːd]
동 성공하다 ✿ succeed in ~에 성공하다
Jake succeeded in swimming across the river.
Jake는 강을 가로질러 헤엄치는 데에 성공했다.

20 weed [wiːd]
명 잡초
Let's pull out the weeds in the field.
밭에 있는 잡초를 뽑자.

Daily Test

A 우리말 뜻과 일치하도록 빠진 글자를 써넣어 단어를 완성하세요.

1 넘다, 초과하다　　__ __ c __ __ d

2 속도　　__ p __ __ d

3 잡초　　__ __ __ d

4 정말, 참으로　　__ n __ e __ __

5 먹이를 주다　　f __ __ __

B 다음 영어 단어의 우리말 뜻을 쓰세요.

1 greed　　_______________

2 seed　　_______________

3 bleed　　_______________

4 succeed　　_______________

5 need　　_______________

C 우리말 뜻과 일치하도록 빈칸에 알맞은 단어를 써넣어 문장을 완성하세요.

1 What time should I _______________ the horses?
내가 몇 시에 그 말들에게 먹이를 줘야 하니?

2 Her forehead is _______________.
그녀의 이마에서 피가 나고 있다.

3 She is driving the bus at low _______________.
그녀는 낮은 속도로 버스를 운전하고 있다.

4 Which tool does the carpenter _______________?
그 목수는 어느 도구가 필요하니?

5 We have to control our _______________.
우리는 욕심을 제어해야 한다.

6 Jake _______________ in swimming across the river.
Jake는 강을 가로질러 헤엄치는 데에 성공했다.

7 The price will not _______________ 50 dollars.
그 가격은 50달러를 넘지 않을 것이다.

8 These _______________ will grow into sunflowers.
이 씨앗들은 자라서 해바라기가 될 것이다.

01	**bright** [brait]	혱 밝은 It was bright and sunny yesterday. 어제는 밝고 화창했다.
02	**delight** [diláit]	몡 기쁨 The boys were shouting with delight. 그 소년들은 기뻐서 소리 지르고 있었다.
03	**fight** [fait]	통 싸우다　몡 싸움　✿ fight-fought-fought Don't fight with your friend again. 다시는 너의 친구와 싸우지 마.
04	**flight** [flait]	몡 비행, 항공편 The flight to New York was canceled. 뉴욕으로 가는 항공편이 취소되었다.
05	**knight** [nait]	몡 기사 Is the knight hurrying to the castle? 그 기사는 그 성으로 급히 가고 있니?
06	**light** [lait]	몡 빛, 불　혱 밝은 Turn on the light when you read a book. 책을 읽을 때는 불을 켜.
07	**night** [nait]	몡 밤 Did Paul make a wish last night? Paul은 어젯밤에 소원을 빌었니?
08	**right** [rait]	혱 오른쪽의, 옳은 My right ear hurts badly. 나의 오른쪽 귀가 몹시 아프다.
09	**sight** [sait]	몡 시력, 보기 My brother has very good sight. 나의 오빠는 시력이 매우 좋다.
10	**tight** [tait]	혱 꽉 조이는 This T-shirt is tight for me. 이 티셔츠는 나에게는 꽉 조인다.

Daily Test

A 우리말 뜻과 일치하도록 빠진 글자를 써넣어 단어를 완성하세요.

1 기쁨   d _ _ _ g _ t

2 기사   _ _ i _ _ t

3 꽉 조이는   _ i _ _ _

4 오른쪽의, 옳은   r _ g _ _

5 싸우다; 싸움   f _ _ h _

B 다음 영어 단어의 우리말 뜻을 쓰세요.

1 light   _________________

2 night   _________________

3 bright   _________________

4 sight   _________________

5 flight   _________________

C 우리말 뜻과 일치하도록 빈칸에 알맞은 단어를 써넣어 문장을 완성하세요.

1 My brother has very good _________________.
나의 오빠는 시력이 매우 좋다.

2 Is the _________________ hurrying to the castle?
그 기사는 그 성으로 급히 가고 있니?

3 Did Paul make a wish last _________________?
Paul은 어젯밤에 소원을 빌었니?

4 Don't _________________ with your friend again.
다시는 너의 친구와 싸우지 마.

5 This T-shirt is _________________ for me.
이 티셔츠는 나에게는 꽉 조인다.

6 The _________________ to New York was canceled.
뉴욕으로 가는 항공편이 취소되었다.

7 My _________________ ear hurts badly.
나의 오른쪽 귀가 몹시 아프다.

8 Turn on the _________________ when you read a book.
책을 읽을 때는 불을 켜.

11	**behind** [biháind]	전 ~ 뒤에 Who is the girl behind you? 너의 뒤에 있는 소녀는 누구니?
12	**bind** [baind]	동 묶다　✿ bind-bound-bound He is binding the letters with a ribbon. 그는 리본으로 그 편지들을 묶고 있다.
13	**blind** [blaind]	형 눈이 먼, 시각 장애가 있는 These books are for blind people. 이 책들은 시각 장애인들을 위한 것이다.
14	**find** [faind]	동 찾다, 발견하다　✿ find-found-found Nick finds a hole in the glove. Nick은 장갑에 난 구멍을 발견한다.
15	**grind** [graind]	동 빻다, 갈다　✿ grind-ground-ground Will the old lady grind coffee? 그 노부인은 커피를 갈 거니?
16	**kind** [kaind]	형 친절한, 다정한 The kind host gave us breakfast. 그 친절한 주인은 우리에게 아침 식사를 주었다.
17	**mankind** [mæ̀nkáind]	명 인류 When did mankind start using fire? 인류는 언제 불을 사용하기 시작했니?
18	**mind** [maind]	명 마음, 생각 She won't change her mind. 그녀는 마음을 바꾸지 않을 것이다.
19	**remind** [rimáind]	동 상기시키다 The photo reminded him of the day. 그 사진은 그에게 그 날을 상기시켰다.
20	**unkind** [ʌnkáind]	형 불친절한, 박정한 He was very unkind to the kids. 그는 그 아이들에게 매우 불친절했다.

A 우리말 뜻과 일치하도록 빠진 글자를 써넣어 단어를 완성하세요.

1 찾다, 발견하다   __ __ n __

2 눈이 먼, 시각 장애가 있는   __ l __ n __

3 묶다   __ __ __ d

4 불친절한, 박정한   u __ __ i __ __

5 인류   m __ __ k __ __ __

B 다음 영어 단어의 우리말 뜻을 쓰세요.

1 grind   ________________

2 remind   ________________

3 kind   ________________

4 behind   ________________

5 mind   ________________

C 우리말 뜻과 일치하도록 빈칸에 알맞은 단어를 써넣어 문장을 완성하세요.

1 Will the old lady ________________ coffee?
그 노부인은 커피를 갈 거니?

2 When did ________________ start using fire?
인류는 언제 불을 사용하기 시작했니?

3 The ________________ host gave us breakfast.
그 친절한 주인은 우리에게 아침 식사를 주었다.

4 The photo ________________ him of the day.
그 사진은 그에게 그 날을 상기시켰다.

5 Nick ________________ a hole in the glove.
Nick은 장갑에 난 구멍을 발견한다.

6 She won't change her ________________.
그녀는 마음을 바꾸지 않을 것이다.

7 Who is the girl ________________ you?
너의 뒤에 있는 소녀는 누구니?

8 He was very ________________ to the kids.
그는 그 아이들에게 매우 불친절했다.

01 alone
[əlóun]

형 혼자인   부 혼자
He enjoys traveling alone.
그는 혼자 여행하는 것을 즐긴다.

02 bone
[boun]

명 뼈
Did he find a real dinosaur's bone?
그는 진짜 공룡 뼈를 발견했니?

03 cone
[koun]

명 원뿔, (아이스크림) 콘
He put strawberry ice cream in a cone.
그는 콘에 딸기 아이스크림을 넣었다.

04 earphone
[íərfòun]

명 이어폰
John took off his earphones.
John은 그의 이어폰을 뺐다.

05 stone
[stoun]

명 돌
The statue was made out of stone.
그 조각상은 돌로 만들어졌다.

06 telephone
[téləfòun]

명 전화, 전화기
The woman should fix her telephone.
그 여자는 그녀의 전화기를 고치는 것이 좋겠다.

07 throne
[θroun]

명 왕좌, 왕위
She came to the throne in 1558.
그녀는 1558년에 왕위에 올랐다.

08 tone
[toun]

명 말투, 어조
The teacher told me in a friendly tone.
그 선생님은 상냥한 어조로 나에게 말했다.

09 xylophone
[záiləfòun]

명 실로폰
Nobody can play the xylophone.
아무도 실로폰을 칠 수 없다.

10 zone
[zoun]

명 지역, 구역
A visitor must not enter this zone.
방문객은 이 구역에 들어가면 안 된다.

Daily Test

A 우리말 뜻과 일치하도록 빠진 글자를 써넣어 단어를 완성하세요.

1 돌   __ t __ n __

2 혼자인; 혼자   __ l o __ __ __

3 원뿔, (아이스크림) 콘   c __ __ __

4 지역, 구역   __ __ __ e

5 전화, 전화기   __ __ __ __ p __ __ n __

B 다음 영어 단어의 우리말 뜻을 쓰세요.

1 bone   ___________

2 earphone   ___________

3 tone   ___________

4 xylophone   ___________

5 throne   ___________

C 우리말 뜻과 일치하도록 빈칸에 알맞은 단어를 써넣어 문장을 완성하세요.

1 The statue was made out of ________________.
그 조각상은 돌로 만들어졌다.

2 Did he find a real dinosaur's ________________?
그는 진짜 공룡 뼈를 발견했니?

3 She came to the ________________ in 1558.
그녀는 1558년에 왕위에 올랐다.

4 He enjoys traveling ________________.
그는 혼자 여행하는 것을 즐긴다.

5 The teacher told me in a friendly ________________.
그 선생님은 상냥한 어조로 나에게 말했다.

6 The woman should fix her ________________.
그 여자는 그녀의 전화기를 고치는 것이 좋겠다.

7 A visitor must not enter this ________________.
방문객은 이 구역에 들어가면 안 된다.

8 He put strawberry ice cream in a ________________.
그는 콘에 딸기 아이스크림을 넣었다.

11 before
[bifɔ́ːr]

전 전에   접 ~하기 전에
Come back home before it starts to rain.
비가 내리기 전에 집에 돌아와.

12 chore
[tʃɔːr]

명 (일상적인) 일
Cleaning is my favorite house chore.
청소는 내가 가장 좋아하는 집안일이다.

13 core
[kɔːr]

명 중심부, 핵심
I want to study about the earth's core.
나는 지구의 중심부에 대해 공부하고 싶다.

14 explore
[iksplɔ́ːr]

동 탐험하다
Her dream is to explore the universe.
그녀의 꿈은 우주를 탐험하는 것이다.

15 ignore
[ignɔ́ːr]

동 무시하다
They ignored our advice.
그들은 우리의 충고를 무시했다.

16 more
[mɔːr]

형 더 많은   부 더 (많이)
Which game is more interesting?
어느 게임이 더 재미있니?

17 score
[skɔːr]

명 득점, 점수
The kid got a perfect score on the test.
그 아이는 시험에서 만점을 받았다.

18 shore
[ʃɔːr]

명 해안
The waves move starfish to the shore.
그 파도는 불가사리들을 해안으로 옮긴다.

19 sore
[sɔːr]

형 아픈, 따가운
I have a sore throat.
나는 목이 아프다.

20 store
[stɔːr]

명 가게
There are fifty stores in the large mall.
그 큰 쇼핑몰 안에는 가게가 50개 있다.

Daily Test

A 우리말 뜻과 일치하도록 빠진 글자를 써넣어 단어를 완성하세요.

1 더 많은; 더 (많이)   m __ __ e

2 (일상적인) 일   __ h __ r __

3 아픈, 따가운   __ __ r __

4 가게   __ t o __ __

5 중심부, 핵심   c __ __ __

B 다음 영어 단어의 우리말 뜻을 쓰세요.

1 shore   _________________

2 score   _________________

3 ignore   _________________

4 explore   _________________

5 before   _________________

C 우리말 뜻과 일치하도록 빈칸에 알맞은 단어를 써넣어 문장을 완성하세요.

1 I want to study about the earth's _________________.
나는 지구의 중심부에 대해 공부하고 싶다.

2 Which game is _________________ interesting?
어느 게임이 더 재미있니?

3 They _________________ our advice.
그들은 우리의 충고를 무시했다.

4 There are fifty _________________ in the large mall.
그 큰 쇼핑몰 안에는 가게가 50개 있다.

5 Her dream is to _________________ the universe.
그녀의 꿈은 우주를 탐험하는 것이다.

6 The waves move starfish to the _________________.
그 파도는 불가사리들을 해안으로 옮긴다.

7 Come back home _________________ it starts to rain.
비가 내리기 전에 집에 돌아와.

8 Cleaning is my favorite house _________________.
청소는 내가 가장 좋아하는 집안일이다.

A 우리말 뜻에 해당하는 영어 단어를 찾아 동그라미 하세요.

자리, 좌석	묶다	오른쪽의, 옳은	말투, 어조	꼬리
실패하다	먹이를 주다	계속 ~이다	득점, 점수	혼자인; 혼자

t	a	i	l	v	b	y	z	l	a
d	v	h	y	b	i	f	a	i	l
r	e	m	a	i	n	p	k	r	o
s	i	z	x	w	d	f	h	h	n
u	v	g	s	n	c	s	e	j	e
w	r	q	h	r	w	e	v	e	j
q	p	b	c	t	j	a	s	c	d
s	c	o	r	e	j	t	o	n	e

B 우리말 뜻과 일치하도록 알맞은 단어를 골라 문장을 완성하세요.

tight	core	unkind	heat	before	contains

1 The ________________ melted the snow.
그 열이 눈을 녹였다.

2 A tomato ________________ much water.
토마토에는 많은 수분이 들어 있다.

3 He was very ________________ to the kids.
그는 그 아이들에게 매우 불친절했다.

4 Come back home ________________ it starts to rain.
비가 내리기 전에 집에 돌아와.

5 This T-shirt is ________________ for me.
이 티셔츠는 나에게는 꽉 조인다.

6 I want to study about the earth's ________________.
나는 지구의 중심부에 대해 공부하고 싶다.

Day 35_C

C 들려 주는 영어 단어를 바르게 쓴 다음, 우리말 뜻을 써넣으세요.

	영어 단어	우리말		영어 단어	우리말
1			11		
2			12		
3			13		
4			14		
5			15		
6			16		
7			17		
8			18		
9			19		
10			20		

D 우리말 뜻과 일치하도록 알맞은 단어를 골라 동그라미 하세요.

1 The (flight / fight) to New York was canceled.
뉴욕으로 가는 항공편이 취소되었다.

2 They work at a (retail / trail) store.
그들은 소매점에서 일한다.

3 She is driving the bus at low (indeed / speed).
그녀는 낮은 속도로 버스를 운전하고 있다.

4 She came to the (tone / throne) in 1558.
그녀는 1558년에 왕위에 올랐다.

5 Our parents (treat / cheat) us all the same.
우리 부모님은 우리를 똑같이 대하신다.

6 Which (pain / train) leaves earlier?
어느 기차가 더 일찍 출발하니?

E 영어는 우리말로, 우리말은 영어로 바꿔 쓰세요.

1	weed	_______________	**2**	인류	_______________
3	rain	_______________	**4**	주된	_______________
5	bone	_______________	**6**	찾다, 발견하다	_______________
7	bright	_______________	**8**	무시하다	_______________
9	jail	_______________	**10**	먹다	_______________
11	sore	_______________	**12**	넘다, 초과하다	_______________
13	night	_______________	**14**	이어폰	_______________
15	repeat	_______________	**16**	항해하다; 돛	_______________
17	indeed	_______________	**18**	싸우다; 싸움	_______________
19	brain	_______________	**20**	지역, 구역	_______________

Day 35_F

F 잘 듣고, 빈칸에 알맞은 단어를 써넣어 문장을 완성하세요.

1 I bite my _______________ when I'm nervous.

2 The woman should fix her _______________.

3 Will the old lady _______________ coffee?

4 Do you know the name of the _______________?

5 Jake _______________ in swimming across the river.

6 Turn on the _______________ when you read a book.

7 _______________ in the exam isn't fair.

8 These books are for _______________ people.

G 우리말 뜻과 일치하도록 빈칸에 알맞은 단어를 써넣어 문장을 완성하세요.

1   Nobody can play the x________________.
아무도 실로폰을 칠 수 없다.

2   A s________________ has a hard shell on its back.
달팽이는 등에 단단한 껍데기가 있다.

3   The woman is cutting m________________ with a knife.
그 여자는 칼로 고기를 자르고 있다.

4   I read the book a________________.
나는 그 책을 다시 읽었다.

5   These s________________ will grow into sunflowers.
이 씨앗들은 자라서 해바라기가 될 것이다.

6   Her dream is to e________________ the universe.
그녀의 꿈은 우주를 탐험하는 것이다.

7   She won't change her m________________.
그녀는 마음을 바꾸지 않을 것이다.

8   My brother has very good s________________.
나의 오빠는 시력이 매우 좋다.

9   The waves move starfish to the s________________.
그 파도는 불가사리들을 해안으로 옮긴다.

10 Flour is made from w________________.
밀가루는 밀로 만든다.

Review에서 틀린 문제의 영어 단어와 우리말 뜻을 쓴 다음, 영어 단어를 3번씩 쓰세요.

	( )	____________ ____________ ____________
	( )	____________ ____________ ____________
	( )	____________ ____________ ____________
	( )	____________ ____________ ____________
	( )	____________ ____________ ____________

Answer Key

Answer Key

Day 01
p. 8

A 1 childhood 2 boy 3 baby 4 adult
5 gentleman

B 1 어린이 2 나이, 연령 3 세대 4 연세가 드신;
연세 드신 분들 5 소녀, 여자 아이

C 1 gentleman 2 age 3 boy 4 baby
5 adults 6 girl 7 child 8 childhood

Day 01
p. 10

A 1 lady 2 people 3 teenager 4 hero
5 man

B 1 (개개의) 사람, 개인 2 남자, 녀석 3 아이
4 (성인) 여자 5 손님, 투숙객

C 1 lady 2 hero 3 person 4 teenager
5 man 6 people 7 guest 8 woman

Day 02
p. 12

A 1 class 2 board 3 art 4 eraser
5 history

B 1 의자 2 사전 3 지구본 4 분필 5 영어

C 1 art 2 eraser 3 dictionary 4 board
5 history 6 class 7 chairs 8 globe

Day 02
p. 14

A 1 science 2 math 3 subject
4 notebook 5 reading

B 1 교과서 2 듣기 3 자 4 음악 5 사회

C 1 notebook 2 ruler 3 Listening
4 subject 5 science 6 reading
7 social studies 8 Music

Day 03
p. 16

A 1 camera 2 climb 3 fishing 4 game
5 bicycle

B 1 마술, 마법 2 체스 3 취미 4 춤을 추다; 춤
5 즐기다

C 1 climbs 2 hobbies 3 magic
4 dancing 5 chess 6 camera
7 enjoys 8 bicycle

Day 03
p. 18

A 1 relax 2 movie 3 yoga 4 stay
5 shopping

B 1 휴식 2 방문하다; 방문 3 우표
4 파도타기를 하다 5 사진

C 1 shopping 2 yoga 3 rest 4 movie
5 visit 6 stay 7 photo 8 stamps

Day 04
p. 20

A 1 bake 2 cheese 3 food 4 egg
5 butter

B 1 꿀 2 빵 3 사탕 4 시리얼 5 쿠키

C 1 butter 2 bread 3 cheese 4 cereal
5 cookies 6 baked 7 honey 8 candy

Day 04
p. 22

A 1 pizza 2 juice 3 water 4 milk
5 soup

B 1 고기 2 기름 3 스테이크 4 차 5 잼

C 1 soup 2 steak 3 milk 4 water
5 pizza 6 juice 7 jam 8 meat

A

v	r	u	l	e	r	e	s	d	r
l	d	c	h	i	l	d	l	t	c
r	p	t	l	c	n	h	g	y	h
v	p	h	y	v	h	r	v	o	a
c	v	c	o	x	e	b	w	g	i
z	i	c	p	t	r	n	n	a	r
b	r	e	a	d	o	y	n	p	l
m	u	s	i	c	a	n	d	y	j

B 1 people 2 steak 3 camera 4 rest
5 social studies 6 dancing

C

	영어 단어	우리말
1	elderly	연세가 드신; 연세 드신 분들
2	climb	오르다, 올라가다
3	board	칠판
4	subject	학과, 과목
5	enjoy	즐기다
6	textbook	교과서
7	baby	아기
8	cheese	치즈
9	woman	(성인) 여자
10	cookie	쿠키
11	gentleman	신사
12	dictionary	사전
13	butter	버터
14	teenager	십 대
15	surf	파도타기를 하다
16	eraser	지우개
17	meat	고기
18	pizza	피자
19	shopping	쇼핑
20	guest	손님, 투숙객

D 1 adults 2 math 3 tea 4 lady
5 magic 6 guy

E 1 역사 2 generation 3 음식, 식량
4 cereal 5 머무르다 6 stamp
7 (개개의) 사람, 개인 8 English 9 주스
10 fishing 11 체스 12 man 13 분필
14 honey 15 소녀, 여자 아이 16 oil
17 영화 18 notebook 19 소년, 남자 아이
20 art

F 1 visit 2 baked 3 Kids 4 jam
5 childhood 6 milk 7 globe
8 Listening

G 1 soup 2 class 3 game 4 reading
5 age 6 eggs 7 science 8 relax
9 hobbies 10 water

A 1 father 2 grandfather 3 brother
4 husband 5 grandmother

B 1 가족 2 사촌 3 고모, 이모, 숙모 4 딸
5 조부모 (중의 한 명)

C 1 grandmother 2 aunt 3 father
4 family 5 husband 6 cousin
7 daughter 8 grandfather

A 1 son 2 niece 3 twin 4 parent
5 wife

B 1 남자 조카 2 삼촌, 이모부, 고모부 3 친척
4 언니, 누나, 여동생 5 어머니

C 1 niece 2 son 3 twins 4 nephew
5 wife 6 relatives 7 mother 8 sister

Day 07
p. 32

A 1 cherry 2 grape 3 apple 4 fruit
5 corn

B 1 당근 2 양배추 3 바나나 4 가지 5 마늘

C 1 carrot 2 fruits 3 corn 4 cabbage
5 Garlic 6 apples 7 grapes 8 cherries

Day 07
p. 34

A 1 peach 2 mango 3 potato 4 orange
5 mushroom

B 1 파인애플 2 채소 3 레몬 4 양파 5 배

C 1 peach 2 lemons 3 pear 4 mangoes
5 mushroom 6 vegetables 7 pineapple
8 onion

Day 08
p. 36

A 1 horse 2 bear 3 goat 4 giraffe
5 animal

B 1 오리 2 새 3 암탉 4 개구리 5 코끼리

C 1 goat 2 horse 3 bird 4 giraffe
5 ducks 6 elephant 7 hen 8 frog

Day 08
p. 38

A 1 snake 2 lamb 3 zebra 4 lion 5 pig

B 1 원숭이 2 늑대 3 호랑이 4 황소
5 이구아나

C 1 pigs 2 wolf 3 iguana 4 snake
5 ox 6 zebras 7 lamb 8 tiger

Day 09
p. 40

A 1 diary 2 clean 3 drink 4 clothes
5 eat

B 1 외출하다 2 운동하다 3 저녁 식사 4 목욕
5 아침 식사

C 1 bath 2 exercises 3 clean 4 eat
5 clothes 6 diary 7 drink 8 dinner

Day 09
p. 42

A 1 wash 2 pet 3 wear 4 lunch
5 homework

B 1 만나다 2 깨다, 일어나다 3 낮잠
4 (잠을) 자다 5 말하다, 이야기하다

C 1 nap 2 wear 3 homework 4 pet
5 talking 6 lunch 7 sleeps 8 meet

Day 10
p. 43

A

j	p	o	t	a	t	o	x	w	d
f	r	u	i	t	b	p	z	c	i
r	q	q	g	n	j	m	f	o	n
o	f	b	r	o	t	h	e	r	n
g	p	l	q	j	r	y	w	n	e
d	c	j	a	p	d	g	i	r	r
n	a	n	i	m	a	l	f	f	k
m	e	e	t	c	b	l	e	z	f

B 1 nephew 2 grapes 3 zebras
4 breakfast 5 Wake up 6 vegetables

C

	영어 단어	우리말
1	grandfather	할아버지
2	garlic	마늘
3	go out	외출하다

4	sister	언니, 누나, 여동생
5	onion	양파
6	lion	사자
7	diary	일기
8	ox	황소
9	pear	배
10	family	가족
11	iguana	이구아나
12	cousin	사촌
13	tiger	호랑이
14	mango	망고
15	uncle	삼촌, 이모부, 고모부
16	clean	닦다, 청소하다; 깨끗한
17	mother	어머니
18	drink	마시다
19	goat	염소
20	apple	사과

D 1 wear 2 parents 3 bears 4 cherries
5 talking 6 snake

E 1 버섯 2 daughter 3 옷, 의복 4 pig
5 암탉 6 orange 7 아버지 8 eat 9 레몬
10 monkey 11 점심 식사 12 relative
13 낮잠 14 cabbage 15 애완동물
16 bath 17 오리 18 giraffe
19 조부모 (중의 한 명) 20 son

F 1 bananas 2 exercises 3 twins
4 horse 5 sleeps 6 peach
7 grandmother 8 bird

G 1 wolf 2 aunt 3 carrot 4 elephant
5 husband 6 homework 7 washed
8 eggplants 9 niece 10 pineapple

p. 48

A 1 bush 2 grass 3 ant 4 flower
5 butterfly

B 1 벌 2 잠자리 3 메뚜기 4 벌레 5 파리

C 1 bush 2 ant 3 dragonfly 4 bug
5 grass 6 fly 7 grasshopper
8 butterflies

p. 50

A 1 insect 2 leaf 3 tulip 4 rose 5 tree

B 1 식물; 심다 2 백합 3 무당벌레 4 해바라기
5 모기

C 1 mosquito 2 leaves 3 sunflowers
4 tree 5 lily 6 insect 7 roses
8 plant

p. 52

A 1 cool 2 fog 3 cloud 4 hot 5 cold

B 1 맑은 2 쌀쌀한 3 마른, 건조한
4 흐린, 구름이 낀 5 안개가 낀

C 1 cold 2 clear 3 cool 4 dry 5 cloud
6 hot 7 foggy 8 chilly

p. 54

A 1 sunny 2 snowy 3 rain 4 wind
5 storm

B 1 눈; 눈이 오다 2 폭풍우가 몰아치는
3 비가 오는 4 따뜻한 5 바람이 부는

C 1 stormy 2 warm 3 snowy 4 storm
5 windy 6 rainy 7 wind 8 sunny

Day 13

p. 56

A   1 drum   2 listen   3 band   4 cello
    5 guitar

B   1 멜로디, 선율   2 연주회, 콘서트   3 하프
    4 플루트   5 (음악) 클래식의, 고전적인

C   1 cello   2 concert   3 band   4 listen
    5 drum   6 harp   7 classical   8 melody

Day 13

p. 58

A   1 recorder   2 opera   3 violin   4 voice
    5 sing

B   1 피아노   2 노래   3 오케스트라, 관현악단
    4 연주하다   5 트럼펫

C   1 piano   2 violin   3 song   4 sings
    5 voice   6 orchestra   7 play   8 trumpet

Day 14

p. 60

A   1 curtain   2 house   3 gate   4 carpet
    5 bedroom

B   1 초인종, 벨, 벨 소리   2 문   3 정원   4 바닥
    5 욕실

C   1 bedroom   2 door   3 garden   4 bell
    5 house   6 bathroom   7 gate   8 carpet

Day 14

p. 62

A   1 sofa   2 mat   3 kitchen   4 yard
    5 table

B   1 거실   2 오븐   3 냉장고   4 스위치   5 창문

C   1 mat   2 windows   3 sofa   4 refrigerator
    5 yard   6 table   7 kitchen   8 oven

Day 15

p. 63

A

v	l	e	a	f	z	c	w	f	g
c	l	o	u	d	y	l	i	m	u
q	d	l	l	e	l	f	n	s	i
l	t	u	l	i	p	c	d	c	t
g	x	b	t	z	r	l	m	p	a
c	a	g	f	f	l	o	w	e	r
t	c	u	r	t	a	i	n	t	r
f	l	u	t	e	j	p	l	a	y

B   1 grasshopper   2 violin   3 sunny
    4 house   5 bathroom   6 bug

C

	영어 단어	우리말
1	opera	오페라
2	switch	스위치
3	chilly	쌀쌀한
4	carpet	카펫
5	insect	곤충
6	voice	목소리
7	dry	마른, 건조한
8	bush	덤불
9	tree	나무
10	concert	연주회, 콘서트
11	sing	노래를 부르다
12	yard	마당, 뜰
13	kitchen	부엌, 주방
14	storm	폭풍, 폭풍우
15	butterfly	나비
16	classical	(음악) 클래식의, 고전적인
17	snow	눈; 눈이 오다
18	rose	장미
19	garden	정원
20	foggy	안개가 낀

D 1 clear 2 piano 3 ant 4 floor
5 mosquito 6 door

E 1 풀, 잔디 2 cloud 3 오케스트라, 관현악단
4 band 5 비가 오는 6 ladybug 7 창문
8 gate 9 백합 10 hot 11 거실
12 drum 13 시원한 14 dragonfly
15 첼로 16 recorder 17 매트, 깔개
18 sofa 19 식물; 심다 20 cold

F 1 bell 2 sunflowers 3 bees 4 melody
5 bedroom 6 trumpet 7 stormy
8 listen

G 1 warm 2 rained 3 harp 4 fog
5 fly 6 snowy 7 oven 8 windy
9 refrigerator 10 song

Day 16
p. 68

A 1 button 2 dress 3 pocket 4 boots
5 hat

B 1 바지 2 장갑 3 청바지 4 외투, 코트
5 (앞에 챙이 달린) 모자

C 1 buttons 2 boots 3 jeans 4 gloves
5 dress 6 pants 7 coat 8 pocket

Day 16
p. 70

A 1 tie 2 shorts 3 sweater 4 ribbon
5 skirt

B 1 티셔츠 2 운동화 3 셔츠 4 양말 5 신발

C 1 sneakers 2 sweater 3 ribbon 4 skirt
5 T-shirt 6 socks 7 shorts 8 tie

Day 17
p. 72

A 1 fencing 2 boxing 3 coach 4 jog
5 baseball

B 1 배드민턴 2 메달 3 골프
4 (테니스 등의) 코트 5 농구, 농구공

C 1 coach 2 boxing 3 medal
4 Badminton 5 Fencing 6 baseball
7 jogs 8 golf

Day 17
p. 74

A 1 racket 2 score 3 team 4 player
5 soccer

B 1 수영 2 달리다 3 스키 (타기)
4 스케이팅, 스케이트 (타기) 5 테니스

C 1 player 2 soccer 3 score 4 run
5 swimming 6 team 7 Tennis
8 rackets

Day 18
p. 76

A 1 hair 2 ear 3 chin 4 fat
5 handsome

B 1 비슷한; 비슷하게 2 얼굴 3 눈 4 귀여운
5 곱슬곱슬한

C 1 fat 2 alike 3 eye, eye 4 handsome
5 chin 6 face 7 cute 8 hair

Day 18
p. 78

A 1 slim 2 mouth 3 ugly 4 nose 5 tall

B 1 예쁜 2 키가 작은 3 치아, 이빨
4 사랑스러운 5 피부

C 1 pretty 2 mouth 3 skin 4 lovely
5 ugly 6 slim 7 tooth 8 nose

Day 19
p. 80

A 1 angry 2 fear 3 bad 4 fun 5 glad

B 1 감정, 느낌, 기분 2 지루해하는 3 울다
4 신이 난, 흥분한 5 두려워하는

C 1 cry 2 angry 3 excited 4 bored
5 afraid 6 fun 7 fear 8 bad

Day 19
p. 82

A 1 laugh 2 joy 3 sorry 4 sad
5 interested

B 1 원하다 2 행복한, 만족스러운 3 초조해하는
4 몹시 화가 난, 미친 5 몹시 싫어하다, 미워하다

C 1 laughing 2 sad 3 hate 4 happy
5 nervous 6 want 7 interested 8 mad

Day 20
p. 83

A

b	u	t	t	o	n	g	f	k	s
b	j	s	w	i	m	m	i	n	g
v	o	y	d	f	h	w	z	w	h
x	g	s	h	i	r	t	n	h	s
c	u	t	e	g	s	r	g	g	l
r	h	z	k	w	w	u	j	s	i
y	j	d	r	q	a	t	e	a	m
c	b	y	s	l	d	c	o	a	t

B 1 gloves 2 fear 3 nose 4 happy
5 baseball 6 shoes

C

	영어 단어	우리말
1	pants	바지
2	sorry	유감스러운, 미안한
3	badminton	배드민턴
4	tennis	테니스
5	skin	피부
6	bad	안 좋은, 나쁜
7	skirt	치마
8	glad	기쁜, 반가운
9	face	얼굴
10	run	달리다
11	fencing	펜싱
12	alike	비슷한; 비슷하게
13	lovely	사랑스러운
14	joy	기쁨, 환희
15	feeling	감정, 느낌, 기분
16	ugly	못생긴, 보기 싫은
17	boxing	권투, 복싱
18	T-shirt	티셔츠
19	ribbon	리본
20	hat	모자

D 1 medal 2 short 3 tooth 4 sweater
5 nervous 6 hate

E 1 부츠, 장화 2 handsome 3 눈 4 jeans
5 골프 6 want 7 곱슬곱슬한 8 coach
9 양말 10 interested 11 머리카락, 털
12 skiing 13 몹시 화가 난, 미친 14 tall
15 스케이팅, 스케이트 (타기) 16 shorts
17 지루해하는 18 afraid 19 주머니
20 player

F 1 fun 2 tie 3 score 4 sneakers
5 court 6 ears 7 chin 8 cap

G 1 excited 2 dress 3 basketball
4 angry 5 soccer 6 sad 7 mouth
8 rackets 9 fat 10 pretty

Day 21

p. 88

A 1 fresh 2 loud 3 noise 4 feel
5 delicious

B 1 ~해 보이다 2 맛 3 맛이 짠 4 듣다
5 맛이 쓴

C 1 heard 2 felt 3 loud 4 delicious
5 salty 6 noise 7 fresh 8 look

Day 21

p. 90

A 1 sense 2 sweet 3 touch 4 sour
5 see

B 1 ~ 냄새가 나다; 냄새 2 맛; ~ 맛이 나다
3 소리 4 (코를 킁킁거리며) 냄새를 맡다
5 매운, 맛이 강한

C 1 sniffing 2 spicy 3 see 4 senses
5 Sweet 6 sour 7 touch 8 smell

Day 22

p. 92

A 1 chew 2 fly 3 bite 4 catch 5 dive

B 1 기다 2 박수를 치다 3 튀다, 튀기다
4 (물 위나 공중에서) 떠가다 5 굽히다, 구부리다

C 1 chew 2 dived 3 clapped 4 bounced
5 Bend 6 flying 7 catch 8 crawl

Day 22

p. 94

A 1 roll 2 jump 3 throw 4 hang 5 kick

B 1 잡고 있다, 들고 있다 2 지나가다
3 두드리다, 노크하다 4 때리다, 치다
5 한 발로 깡충깡충 뛰다

C 1 hit 2 knocked 3 holding 4 rolling
5 pass 6 hang 7 hopping 8 throwing

Day 23

p. 96

A 1 color 2 dye 3 design 4 brush
5 express

B 1 (연필 등으로) 그리다 2 점토, 찰흙
3 형형색색의, 다채로운 4 접다 5 크레용

C 1 clay 2 draws 3 colorful 4 dyed
5 crayons 6 color 7 folded 8 design

Day 23

p. 98

A 1 paper 2 picture 3 tear 4 paste
5 sketchbook

B 1 가위 2 풀, 접착제 3 포스터, 벽보 4 조각상
5 페인트, 그림물감; (그림물감으로) 그리다

C 1 pasting 2 poster 3 glue
4 sketchbook 5 picture 6 tearing
7 statue 8 scissors

Day 24

p. 100

A 1 arm 2 finger 3 blood 4 hand
5 bone

B 1 가슴 2 발 3 몸, 신체 4 뇌 5 팔꿈치

C 1 chest 2 body 3 finger 4 brain
5 bones 6 elbow 7 blood 8 arms

Day 24

p. 102

A 1 wrist 2 heart 3 nail 4 toe 5 neck

B 1 머리 2 무릎 3 어깨 4 허리 5 다리

C 1 nail 2 knee 3 head 4 neck 5 wrist
6 heart 7 shoulder 8 leg

p. 103

A

g	c	s	t	a	t	u	e	r	g
q	b	i	t	e	h	j	n	c	m
s	n	c	n	t	r	q	l	m	v
w	l	o	u	d	o	f	o	o	t
f	r	z	x	k	w	o	o	p	f
d	l	i	x	r	b	l	k	z	r
h	j	k	s	q	t	d	j	l	n
h	e	a	r	t	p	s	o	u	r

B　1 spicy　2 bounced　3 crayons　4 finger
5 heard　6 bones

C

	영어 단어	우리말
1	bitter	맛이 쓴
2	hang	걸다, 매달다
3	chest	가슴
4	see	보다
5	paste	붙이다
6	draw	(연필 등으로) 그리다
7	body	몸, 신체
8	kick	(발로) 차다
9	shoulder	어깨
10	touch	만지다
11	catch	잡다
12	clay	점토, 찰흙
13	tear	찢다, 뜯다
14	fresh	신선한
15	hold	잡고 있다, 들고 있다
16	knee	무릎
17	sound	소리
18	express	표현하다
19	crawl	기다
20	paint	페인트, 그림물감; (그림물감으로) 그리다

D　1 senses　2 toes　3 rolling
4 sketchbook　5 hands　6 design

E　1 형형색색의, 다채로운　2 bend　3 점프하다
4 glue　5 머리　6 feel　7 그림, 사진　8 hit
9 맛이 짠　10 sweet　11 박수를 치다
12 dye　13 (물 위나 공중에서) 떠가다
14 waist　15 목　16 blood
17 두드리다, 노크하다　18 paper
19 ~ 냄새가 나다; 냄새　20 brain

F　1 flying　2 poster　3 flavor　4 noise
5 nail　6 tastes　7 pass　8 color

G　1 arms　2 delicious　3 brush　4 chew
5 sniffing　6 elbow　7 dived　8 leg
9 hopping　10 scissors

p. 108

A　1 cube　2 arrow　3 black　4 purple
5 green

B　1 갈색; 갈색의　2 분홍색; 분홍색의
3 파란색; 파란　4 회색; 회색의　5 원형, 동그라미

C　1 blue　2 black　3 cube　4 pink
5 brown　6 arrows　7 purple　8 green

p. 110

A　1 white　2 shape　3 star　4 round
5 red

B　1 정사각형　2 노란색; 노란색의
3 똑바로; 곧은, 똑바른　4 삼각형　5 직사각형

C　1 square　2 round　3 straight
4 rectangle　5 shape　6 yellow
7 triangle　8 red

Day 27
p. 112

A 1 thirteen 2 twenty 3 sixteen 4 twelve 5 nineteen

B 1 11, 열하나 2 15, 열다섯 3 18, 열여덟 4 14, 열넷 5 17, 열일곱

C 1 twenty 2 twelve 3 sixteen 4 eighteen 5 eleven 6 seventeen 7 fifteen 8 Thirteen

Day 27
p. 114

A 1 seventy 2 number 3 forty 4 hundred 5 fifty

B 1 60, 예순 2 30, 서른 3 1,000, 천 4 80, 여든 5 90, 아흔

C 1 seventy 2 Thirty 3 thousand 4 forty 5 ninety 6 fifty 7 number 8 eighty

Day 28
p. 116

A 1 dish 2 glass 3 fork 4 basket 5 bowl

B 1 망치 2 담요 3 젓가락 4 병 5 컵, 잔

C 1 bowl 2 fork 3 basket 4 cup 5 blankets 6 glass 7 chopsticks 8 hammers

Day 28
p. 118

A 1 jar 2 ladder 3 towel 4 soap 5 knife

B 1 우산 2 열쇠 3 숟가락 4 램프 5 선반

C 1 ladder 2 umbrella 3 soap 4 key

5 towel 6 knife 7 spoon 8 lamp

Day 29
p. 120

A 1 baker 2 doctor 3 artist 4 job 5 actor

B 1 여배우 2 무용수 3 요리사 4 농부 5 디자이너

C 1 actor 2 artist 3 dancer 4 farmers 5 jobs 6 designer 7 cook 8 actress

Day 29
p. 122

A 1 teacher 2 nurse 3 model 4 writer 5 singer

B 1 마술사 2 과학자 3 수의사 4 비행기 조종사 5 음악가

C 1 Models 2 magician 3 scientist 4 vet 5 nurses 6 pilot 7 musician 8 singer

Day 30
p. 123

A

t	s	g	z	x	k	f	o	r	k
w	y	q	r	k	c	u	b	e	b
e	h	g	g	e	r	s	f	f	y
l	k	n	i	f	e	z	u	i	a
v	f	u	q	d	u	n	l	f	c
e	q	r	r	j	l	q	a	t	t
w	k	s	h	a	p	e	m	y	o
h	z	e	u	g	t	t	p	l	r

B 1 brown 2 straight 3 designer 4 sixteen 5 bottles 6 ninety

C

	영어 단어	우리말
1	blue	파란색; 파란
2	bowl	그릇
3	yellow	노란색; 노란색의
4	towel	수건
5	sixty	60, 예순
6	model	모델
7	round	둥근, 원형의
8	glass	유리잔
9	cook	요리사
10	eighteen	18, 열여덟
11	key	열쇠
12	job	일, 직업
13	twenty	20, 스물
14	purple	자주색; 자주색의
15	chopsticks	젓가락
16	fourteen	14, 열넷
17	artist	화가, 예술가
18	thousand	1,000, 천
19	vet	수의사
20	star	별 모양

D 1 dancer 2 white 3 seventy 4 ladder
5 teacher's 6 dish

E 1 병, 단지 2 triangle 3 13, 열셋 4 cup
5 원형, 동그라미 6 umbrella 7 제빵사
8 number 9 80, 여든 10 singer 11 선반
12 seventeen 13 마술사 14 gray
15 19, 열아홉 16 spoon 17 정사각형
18 doctor 19 작가 20 thirty

F 1 eleven 2 arrows 3 pink 4 actress
5 hammers 6 basket 7 musician
8 red

G 1 pilot 2 black 3 rectangle 4 fifteen
5 scientist 6 hundred 7 blankets

8 soap 9 farmers 10 forty

Day 31
p. 130

A 1 jail 2 trail 3 fail 4 snail 5 sail

B 1 손톱 2 소매 3 우편, 우편물 4 꼬리
5 난간, 철도 레일

C 1 jail 2 retail 3 mail 4 trail 5 sailed
6 failed 7 snail 8 rail

Day 31
p. 132

A 1 grain 2 train 3 again 4 rain
5 contain

B 1 뇌 2 아픔, 통증 3 계속 ~이다 4 얻다
5 주된

C 1 brain 2 rains 3 main 4 again
5 train 6 grain 7 pain 8 contains

Day 32
p. 134

A 1 wheat 2 neat 3 seat 4 beat 5 eat

B 1 반복하다, 한 번 더 말하다 2 대하다, 취급하다
3 속이다, 부정행위를 하다 4 고기 5 열

C 1 meat 2 beat 3 eat 4 neat
5 wheat 6 Cheating 7 treat 8 heat

Day 32
p. 136

A 1 exceed 2 speed 3 weed 4 indeed
5 feed

B 1 탐욕 2 씨, 씨앗 3 피가 나다, 피를 흘리다
4 성공하다 5 필요로 하다

C 1 feed 2 bleeding 3 speed 4 need

5 greed   6 succeeded   7 exceed

8 seeds

Day 33

p. 138

A   1 delight   2 knight   3 tight   4 right
5 fight

B   1 빛, 불; 밝은   2 밤   3 밝은   4 시력, 보기
5 비행, 항공편

C   1 sight   2 knight   3 night   4 fight
5 tight   6 flight   7 right   8 light

Day 33

p. 140

A   1 find   2 blind   3 bind   4 unkind
5 mankind

B   1 빻다, 갈다   2 상기시키다   3 친절한, 다정한
4 ~ 뒤에   5 마음, 생각

C   1 grind   2 mankind   3 kind   4 reminded
5 finds   6 mind   7 behind   8 unkind

Day 34

p. 142

A   1 stone   2 alone   3 cone   4 zone
5 telephone

B   1 뼈   2 이어폰   3 말투, 어조   4 실로폰
5 왕좌, 왕위

C   1 stone   2 bone   3 throne   4 alone
5 tone   6 telephone   7 zone   8 cone

Day 34

p. 144

A   1 more   2 chore   3 sore   4 store
5 core

B   1 해안   2 득점, 점수   3 무시하다   4 탐험하다

5 전에; ~하기 전에

C   1 core   2 more   3 ignored   4 stores
5 explore   6 shore   7 before   8 chore

Day 35

p. 145

A

t	a	i	l	v	b	y	z	l	a
d	v	h	y	b	i	f	a	i	l
r	e	m	a	i	n	p	k	r	o
s	i	z	x	w	d	f	h	h	n
u	v	g	s	n	c	s	e	j	e
w	r	q	h	r	w	e	v	e	j
q	p	b	c	t	j	a	s	c	d
s	c	o	r	e	j	t	o	n	e

B   1 heat   2 contains   3 unkind   4 before
5 tight   6 core

C

	영어 단어	우리말
1	mail	우편, 우편물
2	behind	~ 뒤에
3	neat	단정한
4	knight	기사
5	trail	오솔길, 산길
6	remind	상기시키다
7	greed	탐욕
8	cone	원뿔, (아이스크림) 콘
9	pain	아픔, 통증
10	more	더 많은; 더 (많이)
11	beat	이기다
12	store	가게
13	rail	난간, 철도 레일
14	kind	친절한, 다정한
15	bleed	피가 나다, 피를 흘리다
16	chore	(일상적인) 일

17	gain	얻다
18	stone	돌
19	delight	기쁨
20	need	필요로 하다

D 1 flight 2 retail 3 speed 4 throne
5 treat 6 train

E 1 잡초 2 mankind 3 비; 비가 오다
4 main 5 뼈 6 find 7 밝은 8 ignore
9 교도소, 감옥 10 eat 11 아픈, 따가운
12 exceed 13 밤 14 earphone
15 반복하다, 한 번 더 말하다 16 sail
17 정말, 참으로 18 fight 19 뇌 20 zone

F 1 nails 2 telephone 3 grind
4 grain 5 succeeded 6 light
7 Cheating 8 blind

G 1 xylophone 2 snail 3 meat
4 again 5 seeds 6 explore 7 mind
8 sight 9 shore 10 wheat

poster	97
potato	33
pretty	77
purple	107

R

racket	73
rail	129
rain	53, 131
rainy	53
reading	13
recorder	57
rectangle	109
red	109
refrigerator	61
relative	29
relax	17
remain	131
remind	139
repeat	133
rest	17
retail	129
ribbon	69
right	137
roll	93
rose	49
round	109
ruler	13
run	73

S

sad	81
sail	129
salty	87
science	13
scientist	121
scissors	97
score	73, 143
seat	133
see	89
seed	135
sense	89
seventeen	111
seventy	113
shape	109
shelf	117
shirt	69
shoes	69
shopping	17
shore	143
short	77
shorts	69
shoulder	101
sight	137
sing	57
singer	121
sister	29
sixteen	111
sixty	113
skating	73
sketchbook	97
skiing	73
skin	77
skirt	69
sleep	41
slim	77
smell	89
snail	129
snake	37
sneakers	69
sniff	89
snow	53
snowy	53
soap	117
soccer	73
social studies	13
socks	69
sofa	61
son	29
song	57
sore	143
sorry	81
sound	89
soup	21
sour	89
speed	135
spicy	89
spoon	117
square	109
stamp	17
star	109
statue	97
stay	17
steak	21
stone	141
store	143
storm	53
stormy	53
straight	109
subject	13
succeed	135
sunflower	49